The
Spiritual Leadership
of a
Parish Priest

On Being Good
and
Good At It

Rev. J. Ronald Knott

The
Spiritual Leadership
of a
Parish Priest

On Being Good
and
Good At It

THE SPIRITUAL LEADERSHIP OF A PARISH PRIEST:
ON BEING GOOD AND GOOD AT IT

Copyright © 2007 by J. Ronald Knott
All rights reserved.

 For information address Sophronismos Press, 1271 Parkway Gardens Court #106, Louisville, Kentucky 40217.

First Printing: September 2007
ISBN 978-0-9668969-9-2

Printed in the United States of America by:

Morris Publishing
3212 East Highway 30
Kearney, NE 68847
1-800-650-7888

Also by J. Ronald Knott

An Encouraging Word: Renewed Hearts, Renewed Church
The Crossroads Publishing Co., 1995 (out of print)

One Heart at a Time: Renewing the Church in the New Millennium
Sophronismos Press, 1999

Sunday Nights: Encouraging Words for Young Adults
Sophronismos Press, 2000

Diocesan Priests in the Archdiocese of Louisville
Archdiocese of Louisville Vocation Office, 2001

Religious Communities in the Archdiocese of Louisville
Archdiocese of Louisville Vocation Office, 2002

For The Record: Encouraging Words for Ordinary Catholics
Sophronismos Press, 2003

Intentional Presbyterates: Claiming Our Common Sense of Purpose as Diocesan Priests
Sophronismos Press, 2003

For The Record II: More Encouraging Words for Ordinary Catholics
Sophronismos Press, 2004

From Seminarian to Diocesan Priest: Managing a Successful Transition
Sophronismos Press, 2004

For The Record III: Still More Encouraging Words for Ordinary Catholics
Sophronismos Press, 2005

For The Record IV: Even More Encouraging Words for Ordinary Catholics
Sophronismos Press, 2006

For The Record V: Yet More Encouraging Words for Ordinary Catholics
Sophronismos Press, 2007

Intentional Presbyterates: The Workbook
Sophronismos Press, 2007

Copies of Father Knott's books can be ordered online at:
www.saintmeinrad.edu/shop

The
Spiritual Leadership
of a
Parish Priest

On Being Good
and
Good At It

Rev. J. Ronald Knott

Sophronismos Press   Louisville, Kentucky

To the monks of Saint Meinrad Archabbey,
who trained me to be a priest (1964-1970),
inspired me as a priest and trusted me to teach
what I have learned about being a priest.

Acknowledgements

I would like to thank Ms. Kathryn Cone, who read this manuscript, edited it and offered valuable constructive criticism and encouragement. I would also like to thank Ms. Lori Massey for formatting the manuscript into a book. I could not have completed this project without them. I would also like to thank Fr. Larry Richardt, who read the manuscript and offered valuable feedback, as well as Fr. Randy Summers, whose hands appear in the cover photo.

*Instead of wasting time showing people
how holy I am, I am challenged
to show people how holy they are.*

*Joseph R. Veneroso, MM
Maryknoll Magazine
May 1966*

Table of Contents

PREFACE

More than a few veteran observers of the church insist that the most pressing need facing Catholicism today is the quality of its priestly leadership.

Fr. Donald B. Cozzens[1]

Obviously, priests are not the only spiritual leaders in the church, but they are nonetheless spiritual leaders *in the forefront* of the church. No priest carries out his spiritual leadership role in isolation — from the bishop, from other priests, from deacons and certainly not from laity — but in collaboration with all of them. Without the spiritual leadership of the laity, the spiritual leadership of priests is unable to achieve its full effectiveness. The right and duty to exercise spiritual leadership is common to all the faithful, clergy and laity.

Because this book focuses on the spiritual leadership of priests, in no way should it be interpreted as a discount of the spiritual leadership of others in the church. The church cannot do without the spiritual leadership of the bishops, priests, deacons *or* laity. In the church, there is a diversity of service but unity of purpose. This book is meant to focus on the spiritual leadership of priests, not discount the spiritual leadership of others in the church.

I have wanted to write this book for a long time, not because I am the most qualified to do so, but because I sense there is a vacuum, a serious lack of material on spiritual leadership, especially material written for those in the seminary, for those who are preparing for ordination to the priesthood and for those who, having been ordained, will soon become pastors in the church for the first time. It may even be helpful to those who have been leading spiritually for a long time, but who are in need of some encouragement or some fresh insights.

There are five specific reasons why I wrote this book. The first reason is that I am becoming more and more convinced that the People of God, above all, want their priests to be spiritual leaders on one hand, but are increasingly disappointed on the other. I say this not because I am cynical, but because I have been in various situations to be able to hear this message: as a priest who specialized in welcoming back fallen-away Catholics for fourteen years, as a vocation director who has visited more than one hundred parishes, as a columnist for my diocese for five years, and as the director of the Saint Meinrad *Institute for Priests and Presbyterates*.

At a recent annual assembly of Louisville priests, piloted by the *Institute for Priests and Presbyterates*, two laypeople presented the results of their informal survey of average Catholics from around the diocese. Assemblies of priests in other dioceses around the country have featured similar presentations.

According to a news report of the event in *The Record*, the Louisville archdiocesan weekly newspaper, dated June 16, 2006, "(Lay people) want their priests to be spiritual leaders; to be available to people; to have a love of Christ and a caring for all people. And they want them to be personable and welcoming. They expect priests to love their jobs; to lead ministries founded on prayer; to give good homilies; to be involved in religious formation of children and adults; to teach the Catholic beliefs; to be part of the parish in which they serve; to be understanding; and to have good leadership and communication skills." *The Record* went on to say, "People realized priests can only be available to minister if they turn over administrative responsibilities in a parish to others, such as laypeople."[2]

The second reason for writing this book is that many priests have already discovered the fact that handing over the administrative duties to others does not mean that all of a sudden they are possessed with extraordinary spiritual leadership skills. It is a lot easier to balance a budget than to inspire a congregation to move to a new level of discipleship. Spiritual leadership is a gift of God, yes, but it is also a skill that needs to be developed.

The third reason for this book is that I teach in a seminary. I would say that our seminaries are doing a fine job with personal spiritual formation, but are still not doing such a great job forming priests-to-be to be spiritual leaders. Graduates leave the seminary having been the recipients of spiritual formation, but without much training on how to lead the spiritual formation of others, how to be spiritual leaders. It is not enough for a parish priest to be holy; he also needs to have the skills to lead others to holiness.

My fourth reason for writing is also related to the fact that I am a seminary staff member. Too many seminary graduates seem to believe that ordination and a Roman collar will make them "leaders" in the church. When they discover that people will not necessarily follow their lead, frustrated and confused as to why people will not do as they say, these newly ordained sometimes resort to ranting and raving about how they ought to be listened to "because I am a priest!" When things go from bad to worse, some have either walked off the job or sought new assignments. Without insight, this pattern is often repeated with the same disastrous results.

Another fact exacerbates this situation. More and more newly ordained are becoming pastors earlier and earlier, often with no time to settle into the role of being a public person, much less into a leadership position. It is unfair, to them and their people, to thrust them into positions of leadership without asking if they have what it takes to be a leader or without offering them help in developing those skills if they have not had an opportunity to do so.

Fifth, and finally, as a seminary staff member teaching a class on the transition out of the seminary and into priesthood, I know there are many new "parish management" resources, but very few resources on "spiritual leadership." These future pastors, indeed priests of all ages, need help in becoming spiritual leaders, not just in name but in fact. The need is great, but the resources are few. This is my contribution to that need.

A NEW DAY
REQUIRES
A NEW WAY

———— ⅋ ————

A NEW DAY
REQUIRES
A NEW WAY

People do not put new wine into old wineskins.
Rather they pour new wine into fresh wineskins,
and both are preserved.

Matthew 9:17

The only priest I knew as a child, growing up in a rural parish, was Father Felix J. Johnson. He was a quintessential 1950s country pastor.

Our parish property was divided in two by the main highway. On one side of the road were the church, rectory and school. On the other side was the parish cemetery. I can still remember regularly seeing Father Johnson, dressed in coveralls and carrying buckets of feed, walking through the cemetery with his sheep following him in anticipation of their next meal. He was a *real* shepherd, as well as a *figurative* one.

Father Johnson was a practical man, a "hands on" kind of pastor. His sheep kept the cemetery mowed clean, and his spring lambs were one of the main entrees at our parish picnic during the summer.

Father Johnson not only designed the school, convent, rectory and parish hall himself, he also laid the bricks on all of them personally. He kept the parish books, maintained the boiler and raised his own vegetable garden. In short, he basically ran the parish by himself.

As hardworking as he was, Father Johnson did not like people all that much. He rushed through Masses and routinely snapped at people during weddings and baptisms. He had a love-hate relationship with the teaching Sisters and went to as few diocesan meetings as possible. As the first seminarian from our parish in twenty years, his last words to me when I went off to the seminary at age thirteen were, "You won't last 'til Christmas!"

I am sure he was a holy priest, at least we considered him so, but he was seriously lacking when it came to the skills of being an effective spiritual leader. He hated to preach and avoided it most of the time. His worst nightmare was to sit down and do anything that smelled of personal spiritual direction. "Go home and say a Rosary," was his answer to every problem presented to him, whether it was spiritual or relational. He was better at giving advice on where to drill a well, as he did for my dad.

The real spiritual leaders of the parish were the teaching Sisters. They taught us about God and how to pray. They prepared us for the celebration of the Sacraments. There always seemed to be a steady stream of people going in and out of the convent after school hours. People were afraid to "ask Father" so they "asked Sister" to "ask Father" *for* them.

If Father Johnson were alive today, with all the talk about giving the management functions of the parish to the laity, I am sure he would be one lost soul. He would not know what to do with himself. He was definitely a priest for his own time.

As a former pastor of four parishes myself, I think of him often, especially in my work of preparing pastors for the future.

In our *Institute for Priests and Presbyterates* at the Saint Meinrad School of Theology, we are scrambling to catch up with the reality that our graduates will be facing immediately after their ordinations. Some will become pastors immediately, and some of them will become pastors of multiple parishes all at once.

While we are doing what we can to prepare them to work with the laity in managing their parishes, what worries me most is what we are *not* doing to prepare them to be spiritual leaders.

Giving away the management functions of a parish does not mean that these young priests will automatically be left with incredible spiritual leadership skills. Just as in the past, it is much easier to build a gym than it is to move a congregation toward deeper discipleship.

Seminaries are doing a great job in the area of personal spirituality, better than was being done in my own time in the same seminary, but being holy priests will not be enough. To be effective pastors, priests today must also have the skills to lead others to holiness.

Overnight, new priests move from being recipients of spiritual formation to directing the spiritual formation of others, individuals as well as communities. Unfortunately, spiritual leadership skills are neither being taught adequately in the seminary nor can they be infused at ordination. A *designated* spiritual leader is not necessarily a *real* spiritual leader. Pastors of the future must not only be *good* personally, but they must also be *good at* spiritual leadership. The thing that we hear most of all from the laity, when they speak at the presbyteral assemblies we are piloting through our *Institute*, is that they want their priests to be competent spiritual leaders.

If more than personal piety is needed by tomorrow's pastors, what, then, is "spiritual leadership?" From all that I have read and from all that I have learned from my own experience as a pastor, I would say that spiritual leadership is influence; it is the ability of one person to influence others through invitation, persuasion and example, to move from where they are to where God wants them to be. The priest is a bridge to God and never, God forbid, an obstacle to God.

Spiritual leadership is a call from God. Therefore, real spiritual leadership is conducted in a self-effacing, encouraging, quiet, unobtrusive, sympathetic and merciful way. A real spiritual leader lives the words written about Jesus: "A bruised reed he shall not break, and a smoldering wick he shall not snuff out" (Isaiah 42:3.)

A true spiritual leader never gives in to pessimism and hopelessness because he knows that God has already seen to it that the end will be victorious.

True spiritual leaders never abandon people they lead because they refuse to follow or blame them when they do not do the things asked of them. Rather, they step back and work on their skills to influence, induce and mobilize. Good intentions are not enough. The true test of leadership is whether people follow. Ranting and raving about how one ought to be listened to is a sure sign that one is no longer leading spiritually.

A true leader can handle rejection. Although rejection can be a sign that the leader is on the right path, it also can be a sign of serious personality defects. True spiritual leaders are honest with themselves and welcome the honest feedback of others. It is the only way to grow in spiritual leadership ability.

In parish ministry, the personal holiness of a spiritual leader is not enough, but spiritual leadership is impossible without it. What seminaries are doing in the area of personal spirituality is to be commended, but they need to be challenged to include spiritual leadership training in their spiritual formation programs if they hope to form effective spiritual leaders, as well as holy priests.

If there is a pressing need for future pastors to be spiritual leaders, and it is the seminary's job to begin the process of equipping them, there are two essential questions to explore. Can spiritual leadership be taught, and if so, how? What is best taught during the *initial* formation of the seminary, and what is best taught during *ongoing* formation after seminary?

Spiritual leadership is both a gift from God and a skill to be honed. Even if it cannot be taught like a church history class, it can be modeled, studied and emulated. Seminarians would benefit by regular exposure to the great spiritual leaders of our church's long history, as well as the spiritual leaders of other faith communities — an in-depth study of how the great spiritual leaders of the past did what they did. This richer vision of spiritual formation could include witness talks from those who are leading effectively in our own day. It is helpful to study success stories.

The platforms from which the spiritual leadership of a diocesan priest is practiced are the pulpit, the presider's chair and the designated leadership role given to him by his bishop. Diocesan priests are preachers of the Word, ministers of the sacraments and leaders of faith communities. They cannot be effective spiritual leaders without honing these three skills.

Parish preaching has been called "group spiritual direction from the pulpit." Homiletics has greatly improved in seminaries, but more work needs to be done in teaching these young, busy pastors how to organize their homiletic work within a busy schedule. "Wallowing in the Word," in preparation to preach, could become the foundation of a diocesan priest's spirituality, not just one of a hundred things to do.

Preaching and presiding at the celebration of the Sacraments are one and the same: proclamation of Good News. Both are invitations seeking a response. In the Vatican II church, at long last, they have been wedded like never before. Therefore, a priest who wants to be an effective spiritual leader could benefit from knowing the Sacramentary and Rituals from top to bottom. Studying them is a source of continuous personal spiritual growth as well as sacred tools to lead others to holiness. Familiarizing oneself with these tools before presiding at the celebration of the sacraments is an essential step in effective spiritual leadership.

Priests act *in persona Christi,* in spite of their own personal weaknesses. Even though the message does not depend on the goodness of the messenger, priests need to continuously hone their skills for communicating the goodness of the message. Of special importance is the capacity to relate to others so as to be a "bridge" for communicating Jesus Christ. This is the purpose of human formation that begins in the seminary. Likewise, a high standard of ceremony and liturgical celebration, free from spectacle and personal tastes for styles foreign to the church, must be taught and embraced, beginning in the seminary.

Some priests could be more effective. There is a world of difference between *being a priest* and *priesting*. The seminary process is often focused on getting ordained. The question that every priest-to-be could to ask himself, especially at the end, is this: "Now that I will be a priest, what kind of priest do I will to be?" A priest needs to *priest* and do it well!

Seminary is not enough. Maybe it has never been, but this observation is certainly true these days. Long-term preparation for ongoing formation, both awakening a desire for it and seeing its necessity, needs to take place in the seminary; after seminary, it needs to continue for the rest of a priest's life.

Ongoing formation is an intrinsic requirement of the gift and sacramental ministry received. It is the bishop's job to see to it that appropriate conditions for its realization are ensured and that his priests take advantage of those opportunities. Excellent spiritual leadership requires it.

Mother Teresa may have put the requirements of spiritual leadership most simply when she said, "To keep a lamp burning you have to keep putting oil in it."

THE RIGHT THING
FOR THE RIGHT
REASON

THE RIGHT THING FOR THE RIGHT REASON

With what rashness, then, would the pastoral office be undertaken by the unfit, seeing that the government of souls is the art of arts. Although those who have no knowledge of the power of drugs shrink from presenting themselves as physicians of the flesh, people who are utterly ignorant of spiritual precepts are often not afraid of professing themselves to be physicians of the heart.

St. Gregory the Great[3]

"Beware of false prophets, who come to you in sheep's clothing, but underneath are ravenous wolves." Matthew 7:15 reflects a problem of Matthew's own time, bad leadership even in the early church. Today, not all who seek spiritual leadership in the church do so for the best reasons. Some (with the possible exception of Catholic priests) are motivated by money; some are motivated by a need for the approval and respect of others. Failing to understand or acknowledge the scars of their past, some end up being more motivated by anger than by love, and still others seek positions of spiritual authority as a means of personal aggrandizement rather than as an avenue to serve God.

"The quality and strength of one's motivation are vital to any lifelong vocation. The temptation to seek priesthood motivated by power, privilege, status and security or to create a feeling of identity can be strong. Other effective motives would be to seek such forms of self-enhancement as comfort, exhibition or unearned affirmation. Likewise are the desires to do social work, to make reparation for an alcoholic father, to satisfy maternal expectations or to cover up a confused psychosexual life. None of these deficit motivational patterns will sustain one for a long time."[4]

Emotionally needy people are especially drawn to the status and practice of ordained ministry. Since it takes humility and vulnerability to do so, some never examine what lies behind their desire to be a leader and are driven by unnamed demons. For this reason, the church needs to take great care to screen out needy people who don't know who they are or who have no insight into their own motivations. If not, the neediness of these individuals can derail even the best parishes in a short time. This neediness can manifest itself in an insatiable need to be the focus of attention and affirmation, an authoritarian leadership style, hasty liturgical changes based on their personal preferences, an inability to listen and a disrespect for what has been done before their arrival. Most, thank God, are driven by a genuine desire to do God's work.

The church today craves and needs good leaders, but at a time when society at large is displaying a growing interest in spiritual issues, there is an acute shortage of good spiritual leaders. The problem is not from a lack of people willing to present themselves as leaders. In fact, "At the heart of America is a vacuum into which self-appointed saviors have rushed."[5] People are so desperate for leaders that they are susceptible to following destructive and delusional gurus; would-be messiahs; almost anyone who promises miracles, signs and wonders; and those who claim to know the truth, the whole truth and nothing but the truth. Most, however, simply endure and wait out run-of-the-mill incompetents, many of whom are arrogant as well as ignorant.

The first caution for beginners in "spiritual leadership" may be: "A designated leader" may or may not be "a real leader." People seem to know intuitively that claiming to be a leader or holding a leadership position does not make someone a leader. Even seminaries are bewildered that so few real leaders are emerging from their graduating classes. God's call and ordination make one a *designated* leader, but whether one becomes a *real* leader is additionally a matter of intention, skill and practice. Good will is not a substitute for competence. A true leader has the ability to unleash the power of individuals and to direct it toward the goals of the community. The Good News, and its communication through word and deed, is what spiritual leadership is all about. Indeed, an ordination, a collar and a title do not necessarily make one an effective spiritual leader. The best scenario is when a designated leader is also a real leader.

One of the most painful lessons I had to learn as a first-time pastor was that having the title of a leader did not necessarily mean that I was, in fact, a leader. I had accepted the title of pastor, but I was ambivalent and unprepared for all that a pastor of an important and visible church like a cathedral needs to be. As a result of my indecision and lack of focus, the associate pastor "took charge" and left me in the dust. Our constant clashes came to a head one day when one of the musicians screamed out at a tense meeting, "The trouble around here is that we have two 'pastors'." It hit me like a ton of bricks: I had the title and the associate had the power. Instead of being angry at him, I decided to step up to the plate and committed myself to becoming a pastor not just in name, but also in fact.

The second caution for beginners in "spiritual leadership" may be: "Know thyself." Father William Moorman, coordinator of spiritual formation at St. Luke Institute, a treatment center for priests, says this about some of our leaders-to-be. As spiritual leaders, "we are entrusted with the unique responsibility of embracing the sacred intimacy of another's spiritual life. Can this be possible if we are unable to embrace the mystery and the sanctity of our own identity? Too often candidates are looking for the identity of priests/religious as a vicarious personal identity, which is always a formula for disaster. Most often these individuals insist on external order to balance their internal chaos, and they never achieve the inner peace they long for in their spiritual lives.

Spirituality for such persons resides outside themselves in spiritual practices, as opposed to embracing the mystery of God, others and self." Any formation program for "spiritual leaders" assumes reasonably integrated individuals, but Father Moorman notes that because of the shortage of seminarians, screening and formation programs are accepting and tolerating candidates with demonstrable personality traits such as dependency, avoidance, narcissism and obsessive/compulsive behavior.[6] Priesthood, even today, offers seductions of power, prestige and flattery. These seductions attract those who are drawn to the status and practice of ministry because it helps to satisfy their need to be the focus of attention and affirmation. This focus becomes even more pernicious if it is couched in the religious language about being servants.

Saint Gregory the Great, in his remarkably applicable work, "Pastoral Care," warns of those who "investigate spiritual precepts with shrewd diligence...but teach what they have learned, not by practice, but by study, and belie in their conduct what they teach by words." As if writing about recent events in our church, he observes, "For no one does more harm in the church than he who, having the title or rank of holiness, acts evilly."[7]

He goes on to warn of those who enter into ministry with a divided heart. "The mind cannot possibly concentrate on the pursuit of any one matter when it is divided among many. It is as though it were so preoccupied during the journey as to forget what its destination was, with the result that it is so great a stranger to the business of self-examination as not to be aware of the harm it suffers, or to be conscious of the great faults it commits."[8]

Saint Gregory the Great, again with remarkable application to a few priests today, warns of those "who...busy themselves with a variety of inquisitions, more than is needful, and fall into error by their excessive subtlety." Fools rush in where angels fear to tread. Rather, he says, "When the ruler prepares to speak, he must bear in mind to exercise a studious caution in his speech, for if his discourse, hastily given, be ill-ordered, the hearts of his hearers may be stricken with the wound of error, and when perhaps, he wishes to appear wise, he will by his lack of wisdom sever the bond of unity."[9] Many unseasoned new pastors have done great damage to the Church in their zeal for, but limited understanding of, "orthodoxy and truth."

The third caution for beginners in "spiritual leadership" may be: *"Nemo dat quod non habet."* "No one gives what he does not have." Saint Gregory Nazianzus put it another way. "Before purifying others, they must purify themselves; before instructing others, they must be instructed; they have to become light in order to illuminate and become close to God in order to sanctify."[10] Indeed, as Father Howard P. Bleichner wrote, "Lofty prose is easily mouthed."[11] It is easy to recite high ideals, but very difficult to live them.

A fourth caution for beginners in "spiritual leadership" may be: "Integrity is essential to leadership." Gregory the Great says, "For one who is so regarded that the people are called his flock must carefully consider how necessary it is for him to maintain a life of rectitude. It is necessary, therefore, that he should be pure in thought, exemplary in conduct, discreet in keeping silence, profitable in speech, in sympathy a near neighbor to everyone, in contemplation exalted above all others, a humble companion to those who lead good lives, erect in his zeal for righteousness against the vices of sinners. He must not be remiss in his care for the inner life by preoccupation with the external; nor must he in his solicitude for what is internal, fail to give attention to the external." He goes on to say, "For one who by the exigency of his position must propose the highest ideals is bound by that same exigency to give a demonstration of those ideals. His voice penetrates the hearts of his hearers the more readily if his way of life commends what he says."[12]

A fifth caution for beginners in "spiritual leadership" may be: "It's not about you!" It has always been true for newly ordained priests, but one of the many down sides of a priest shortage is that the traditional "headiness" that comes with ordination is being exacerbated. Newly ordained priests and priests-to-be are so often "made over" and "focused on" during their days in the seminary and especially during their ordinations and "first masses" that they begin to feel special, maybe too special. This powerful surge of special treatment, unmonitored, can lead quickly to the cocksure arrogance of clericalism and entitlement. As Pope John Paul II put it, priests are not above the laity or alongside the laity, but *for* the laity. It's not about us, but them!

The best advice to those who want to prepare themselves for "spiritual leadership" is to insist that they do serious inner work to see if they have the "right stuff" to practice the art of arts, to be physicians of the heart. Otherwise they ought to be arrested for false advertising or dismissed as a menace to the People of God, even if they do mean well.

SPIRITUAL LEADERSHIP

SPIRITUAL LEADERSHIP[13]

All that matters is that one is being created anew.

Galatians 6:15

If you thought this book was about how to run a parish, about parish management techniques, you were wrong. Spiritual leadership is not the same as parish management, the focus of most books on the practice of ministry in recent years.

A recent e-mail from a female friend in Massachusetts says it all. "Our parish is going to have an opportunity for spiritual growth with (our new pastor), and I could not be happier. (The former pastor) was more of a businessman than a spiritual leader, which was good for building the big complex and paying off the mortgage, but it left so many (spiritually) dry. This change will be good."

Spiritual leadership operates on the emotional and spiritual resources of the organization, on its values, commitments and aspirations. Management, by contrast, operates on the physical resources of the organization, on its capital, human skills, raw materials and technology. As the management guru, Peter Drucker, has said, "Management is doing things right; leadership is about doing the right thing." If that is true, then it is much easier, for example, to balance a budget or build a gym than it is to lead people into a deeper level of discipleship. Leading people into a deeper level of discipleship is what spiritual leadership is all about.

It is not enough for a spiritual leader to be personally holy, even though a person who is responsible for leading others spiritually is assumed to possess holiness in the highest degree. Anyone who accepts responsibility for leading others to holiness needs to have already learned the self-discipline necessary for holiness. *Nemo dat quod non habet.* One cannot give what one does not have.

Having already learned to live a holy life as an individual Christian, spiritual leaders must learn how to exercise authority over other Christians in a way that will be useful to them. Certainly they need to have certain virtues in order to conduct their own lives without reproach, but they also need to have additional virtues: the ability to humbly obey those who exercise leadership over them, as well as the ability to give worthwhile spiritual direction to the people under their care.[14]

Neither is it enough for spiritual leaders to seek holiness, their own or others, as if it were simply quantitative, a set of calculated ascetical and devotional practices that will result in the desired outcome. Spirituality is about embracing the mystery of God in oneself and in others. As Jesus taught the Scribes and Pharisees, real spirituality is about *metanoia*, a change of heart or a new way of thinking, not merely checking off a list of pious practices or simply following the established rules of the church. It's easier to count prayers and display religious conformity than it is to become a "new creation" (Gal 6:15).

What, then, is "spiritual leadership"? Spiritual leadership is ultimately *influence*, the ability of one person to influence another through invitation, persuasion and example to move from where they are to where God wants them to be.

God is working throughout the world to achieve his purposes and to advance his kingdom. God's concern is not to advance leaders' dreams and goals nor to join in their agendas nor to bless their efforts. Neither do spiritual leaders try to satisfy the goals and ambitions of the people they lead, but rather those of the God they serve. Spiritual leaders seek God's will and then marshal the people they lead to do his will.

Leaders may entertain, impress or even motivate people, but if there is no spiritual growth in the people they lead, their leadership comes from the leader's talent, but not necessarily from God. When spiritual leaders have done their jobs, people around them have encountered God and do his will. The spiritual leader's primary task is to work with God to encourage the faith of others.

Spiritual leaders allow God to use them in his work to transform people into better disciples. When someone leads in the Spirit's power, lives are changed. Spiritual leadership is about influence in helping to make Christ real for others.

Unlike secular leadership, which is something to which people can aspire, spiritual leadership is assigned by God. Spiritual leaders are not elected, appointed or created by personnel boards. God alone makes them. One does not become a spiritual leader by merely filling an office, taking course work in the subject or resolving in one's own will to do this task. People do not become spiritual leaders unless God calls them to this role and equips them for it.

Spiritual leadership is far from magic because "grace builds on nature." This means, in part, that a certain level of human effort is necessary in order for grace to do its work of transforming a person chosen by God into a skilled spiritual leader. The Parable of the Talents reminds us that even the gifts God bestows on us must be "invested." God's call to spiritual leadership may be instant, but developing spiritual leadership skills requires years of focused attention and prayer. One does not become a spiritual leader by simply dabbling in it, but through a deliberate intention to master the skills needed. "Intention" comes from the Latin word "*intendere*," meaning to "reach for" or "stretch toward."

One of my favorite quotes on this kind of commitment is from W. H. Murray. "Until one is committed, there is hesitancy, the chance to draw back, always ineffectiveness. Concerning all acts of initiative and creation there is one elementary truth, the ignorance of which kills countless ideas and splendid plans, that at the moment one definitely commits oneself, then Providence moves too. All sorts of things occur to help one that would never otherwise have occurred. A whole stream of events issues from the decision, raising in one's favor all manner of unforeseen incidents and meetings and material assistance, which no man could have dreamed would come his way."[15] Jesus calls *and* equips, but a spiritual leader must answer that call and be skillful in using the equipping that God offers.

Natural leadership qualities are an important component of spiritual leadership. These natural talents may be God-given, but they must be called forth, trained and used for spiritual leadership. In the area that seminaries call "human formation," spiritual leaders need to develop certain qualities that God can build on and work with. They must, among others things, be able to:

- master his appetites
- remain calm in crises and resilient in disappointment
- think independently
- handle criticism
- triumph over set-backs
- demonstrate strength, not power
- reconcile differences
- induce people to do something they would not otherwise do
- take opposition without taking offense
- trust people
- say "thank you"
- make and keep friends
- have an ease in the presence of strangers and superiors
- show an interest in, and a concern for, all types and races of people
- be tactful and steady
- demonstrate an ability to forgive
- be optimistic
- welcome responsibility
- keep a secret
- get over demanding perfection from self and others
- adapt to various audiences
- be above reproach
- enjoy a good reputation
- possess an unquestioned personal morality

- teach
- be actively considerate
- manage his own affairs
- be spiritually mature
- possess a magnanimous spirit and broad vision
- finish a job, especially a difficult job

Even though spiritual leadership is a gift, accepting such a gift is hardly ever easy. "My son, when you come to serve the Lord, prepare yourself for trials" (Sirach 2:1). When God finds a person who is ready to lead, to commit to full discipleship and to take responsibility for others, that person is used to the limit. Because of that, spiritual leadership has always required strength and faith beyond the merely human. Gideon asked God, "How can I do what you have called me to do?" "I will be with you," God answered (cf. Judges 6:15-16). Psalm 80:18 says, "May your help be with the man at your right hand, with the one whom you once made strong."

Spiritual leadership may be difficult, but it is worth the sacrifice. One can find great comfort in the encouraging, yet challenging, words of George Bernard Shaw. "The true joy of life, the being used for a purpose recognized by yourself as a mighty one; the being thoroughly worn out before you are being thrown on the scrap heap; the being a force of nature instead of a feverish, selfish little clod of ailments and grievances complaining that the world will not devote itself to making you happy."[16]

Spiritual leadership, since it is a gift, is neither be strident nor flamboyant. A spiritual leader conducts a ministry that is self-effacing, encouraging, quiet, unobtrusive, sympathetic and merciful. A true spiritual leader lives the words written about Jesus, "A bruised reed he shall not break, and a smoldering wick he shall not snuff out" (Isaiah 42:3).

A true spiritual leader never gives in to pessimism because he knows that God has already seen to it that the end will be victorious. The kingdom *will* come, not because of us, but in spite of us.

True spiritual leaders never abandon those they lead because they refuse to follow or blame them when they do not behave as they should behave. Rather, they step back and work on their skills to influence, induce and mobilize.

Spiritual leaders in name only, people who make no difference in people's lives, are not actually spiritual leaders. Spiritual leadership is ultimately not measured by position or title or even ordination, but results. The test of a spiritual leader is whether those under his care have grown in their discipleship.

As a reaction to the authoritarianism of the pre-Vatican II church, a style of spiritual leadership, leadership from the rear, became popular in the post-Vatican II church. As a result, a sort of abdication of leadership became popular. In reaction, those who crave order and fall apart in the presence of pluralism want to go back to the imagined security of the past.

Why should we have to choose between dictators and wimps? Why not have leaders who exude strength and character? Consultation, consensus building and power sharing are good and even necessary, but a spiritual leader cannot lead from the rear. "If the bugle gives an indistinct sound, who will get ready for battle?" (1 Corinthians 14:8). Spiritual leaders are called to be real leaders, not merely chairpersons.

Vision, and its communication through word and deed, is what pastoral leadership is all about. Pastoral leadership communicates the vision of the kingdom to come constantly: in preaching, in face-to-face conversation and in personal example. The spiritual leader must convince people that he believes the Good News, is excited about it and personally puts it into practice.

The kingdom, here and to come, is the vision. A spiritual leader's task is to inspire people to reach for it, through word and deed. His job is to hold the congregation, without wavering, to the vision of God's kingdom, here and to come. People naturally want to belong to, and support, a church that knows who it is and what God wants it to do.

People want to be challenged and encouraged, not condemned or belittled. They want their vision lifted to higher sights, their performance to a higher level, their personalities stretched beyond normal limitations. Some reasons people leave the church are: not being treated with respect and dignity by church leaders, being prevented from offering their gifts and talents, not being heard, not being given more responsibility.

In reaction to an indiscriminate and uncritical acceptance of secular leadership theory by some church leaders, other church leaders, especially the younger ones, reject any and all secular leadership principles. This is a sad fact because many of the "modern" leadership principles currently being espoused are, in fact, biblical principles. They must be read critically, but much can be learned from them.

Likewise, many young church leaders will not read "Protestant" leadership material. This too is a sad fact, because "some, even very many, of the most significant elements or endowments which together go to build up and give life to the church herself can exist outside the visible boundaries of the Catholic church. Whatever is wrought by the grace of the Holy Spirit in the hearts of our separated brethren can contribute to our own edification."[17] A true spiritual leader will be open to learning from many sources. The truth is the truth no matter who speaks it.

Where do priests begin when they want to improve their spiritual leadership skills? They begin with their own relationship with God. Spiritual leadership ability grows in direct proportion to one's own spiritual growth. As spiritual leaders grow, they increase their capacity to lead. As they increase their capacity to lead, those they lead are empowered to grow proportionately. The best thing spiritual leaders can do for their people is to grow personally. As leaders commit to their own personal growth and learning, they become ever better vehicles for carrying out God's work. Pope John Paul II said it well, "All formation, including priestly formation, is ultimately self-formation."[18]

PRIESTHOOD: A SHARED SPIRITUAL LEADERSHIP

————— ഇ —————

PRIESTHOOD: A SHARED SPIRITUAL LEADERSHIP

All priests are united among themselves in an intimate sacramental brotherhood. For even though priests are assigned to different duties they still carry on one priestly ministry. Hence no priest can in isolation or single handedly accomplish his mission in a satisfactory way. He can do so only by joining forces with other priests under the direction of church authorities.

Presbyterorum Ordinis, 7-8[19]

Priests are not priests simply one by one, but they are priests and serve the mission of the church in a presbyterate in union with the bishop.

Thanks to Vatican Council II, and especially Pope John Paul II, the theology of a presbyterate, often referred to as "an intimate sacramental brotherhood," working as a team under a bishop, has been restored. This ancient theology was strong in the early days of the church but has been neglected for centuries, until our own time. From the New Testament and early Christian writings, we see that the ancient church did not think in terms of solitary priests but of a *presbyterium*. It was a college of priests who surrounded the bishop to help him carry out his ministry.

Why was this idea neglected?[20] (1) With the spread of the church outside the original see cities, after the legalization of Christianity, there was a general breakdown of the early idea of collegiality and a trend toward an *individual*, rather than a *collegiate*, ministry. This physical separation from the city, where the *presbyterium* would meet, limited priests' participation in it. (2) Another historical factor that encouraged individualism was the development of the benefice system and the resulting ministry to a particular church whose benefactor would guarantee a priest's economic sustenance. This contributed to a decline in the common life and collaboration among priests, as they would feel less of a bond to the bishop than they would to their benefactor. (3) Some see an affirmation of individualism coming from the Council of Trent with its emphasis on the character of the individual priest, with a special dignity and personal power to celebrate the Eucharist privately.

With the spread of the church, therefore, the concept of a *presbyteral community*, as well as the meaning of the word *presbyterium* itself, could be said to have been slowly lost through centuries of neglect. The word "neglect" is worthy of emphasis. As was noted above, it was the collapse of a strong idea of *collegial ministry* that gave rise to the practice of *individual ministry* by priests.

In our own time, it is worth noting that it is the bishops themselves who are most articulate in describing this neglect and its resulting problems. In their 2001 *Basic Plan for the Ongoing Formation of Priests*, they say: "A bishop has many responsibilities, and many things claim his attention. Presbyteral unity may not seem to be as pressing, for example, as dealing with individual priests who are problematic, with the distribution and assignment of clergy, or with the recruitment of new candidates. Working for presbyteral unity can slip to a lower end of a list of priorities. In fact, its neglect favors divisions and, ultimately, a number of attendant problems in the diocese."[21]

Without the strong leadership of bishops, who are the heads of diocesan presbyterates, in presenting a unified vision and unleashing the power of the team, many diocesan priests have fallen into the habit of operating like the "Lone Ranger." Because of continuing neglect and the lack of a shared vision, something new and maybe even more destructive is happening. Priests are beginning to form "tribes" within their presbyterates. Without a shared vision, small groups of like-minded priests are left to battle it out over who has the right vision.

Both "priests in private practice" of our recent past, as well as today's growing "tribalism," fly in the face of solid church teaching. "...the priest cannot act by himself; he acts with the presbyterate becoming a brother of all who constitute it."[22] "A priest will therefore make every effort to avoid living his own priesthood in an isolated and subjectivistic way, and must try to enhance fraternal communion..."[23] "...priests are never to put themselves at the service of an ideology or human faction."[24]

Presbyteral unity has been neglected for so long that there is no clear map to follow. Again, it was the bishops themselves who described the situation and the lack of clear direction for the future. "The church continues to deepen her understanding of priestly ministry and life that emerged in the Second Vatican Council; namely, priests are not priests simply one by one, but they are priests and serve the mission of the church in a presbyterate in union with the bishop. The corporate sense of priestly identity and mission, although not fully developed even in official documents, is clearly emerging as an important direction for the future."[25] They, quite wisely, noted the difference between the ongoing formation of individual priests and the ongoing formation of presbyterates. The ongoing formation of individual priests is important, but the ongoing formation of whole presbyterates may be needed even more. *Pastores Dabo Vobis* summarizes Vatican II teaching and offers this simple yet challenging statement: "The ordained ministry has a radical *'communitarian form'* and can only be carried out as collective work."[26]

One respected southwestern bishop said recently that "the most important problem" he faces with priests is "their inability to work with one another." This, sadly, is not just a local problem for him, but a growing problem facing many presbyterates in this country. He not only described a weakness in us priests, but also a major weakness in our bishops in their inability and lack of skill in bringing out the best in our presbyterates.

How can presbyterates, commissioned to be "men of communion," lead a divided church and divided parishes if they are divided among themselves? How can priests lead multi-cultural parishes in a multi-cultural world that is growing more and more multi-religious when they cannot themselves work together? Priests are called to be on the front line of healing divisions in our parishes, in our church and, yes, in our world.

As *The Basic Plan for the Ongoing Formation of Priests* notes, these divisions have significant consequences. Priests have a vocation to be shepherds, pastors of souls to all, regardless of their theological or cultural makeup, orientation or age. If a priest cannot be in communion with his presbyterate, how can he hope to be a "man of communion" for the church? (1) These divisions lead to diminished effectiveness that undermines the utilization of valuable human resources needed to address pressing issues. (2) When these divisions are public, and they usually are, they constitute an anti-sign for the community and discourage those who might feel called to the priesthood. (3) These divisions create loneliness, especially for our newest priests, the biggest factor in so many leaving in their first five years. Those who leave do so because of feelings of loneliness, isolation, being unappreciated and being disconnected. When their presbyterates are more like a "loose association of lone rangers," instead of an "intimate sacramental brotherhood," they are most especially vulnerable to seeking out coupled relationships as a substitute. (4) Finally, divisions can shift the focus of priests from a wide-ranging diocesan perspective to a narrow, localized emphasis on one's own parish with a resultant parochialism.[27]

Coherent and unified presbyterates will not happen by accident, but by intention. The word "intention" comes from the Latin word *intendere*, meaning "to stretch toward, to aim at." Intention is an act of the will by which that faculty efficaciously desires to reach an end by employing the means. It is a concentration of will to the point of resolve. We have to really want it before we can have it.

Like the original twelve apostles, Christ calls his priests to resist those things that threaten the unity of the group — especially working alone, working too much and working against each other (Mark 6:7-12, 30-32; 10:35-45).

Healthy and unified presbyterates cannot happen when each one in it is doing his own thing. Priests in a presbyterate are like an orchestra rather than a loose association of soloists. Saint Ignatius of Antioch, who spoke often of the presbyterate, said, "Your presbytery, which is a credit to its name, is a credit to God; for it harmonizes with the bishop as completely as the strings with a harp."[28] Without leaders to inspire priests and lead them with a common vision, the visions of little cliques will continue to battle each other over who has the "true" vision. A real leader inspires a shared vision and calls individual priests to greatness in translating that vision into reality. To paraphrase Vince Lombardi, "Individual commitment to a group effort — that is what makes a presbyterate work, a company work, a society work, a civilization work."

For the sake of focus and unity, diocesan priests make two solemn promises: celibacy and obedience. Rather than negatives, the promises of celibacy and obedience are meant to free us up for ministry. Priests get extensive formation in celibacy, but not in obedience. Obedience is the neglected stepchild of the priestly promises. Once made, it is often forgotten. Of the two promises, the only one ever heard much about is celibacy, but "that other promise" may be even more important for unified ministry to the People of God.

"Among the virtues most necessary for the priestly ministry must be that disposition of soul by which priests are always ready to seek not their own will, but the will of the one who sent them.[29]

The promise of obedience has implications beyond the relationship of each individual priest to his bishop. Priestly obedience also has a community dimension. It is not the obedience of an individual who alone relates to authority, but rather an obedience that is deeply part of the unity of the presbyterate.[30]

The promise of obedience includes a promise to his fellow presbyteral members. This promise is really a promise to be a "team player" with the bishop *and* the other members of his presbyterate for the sake of the common purpose they share.[31]

This obedience demands a marked spirit of asceticism, both in the sense of a tendency not to be too bound up in one's own preferences or points of view and in the sense of giving brother priests the opportunity to make use of their talents and abilities, setting aside all forms of jealousy, envy and rivalry. Priestly obedience is one of solidarity, based on belonging to a single presbyterate. Within the presbyterate, this obedience is expressed in co-responsibility regarding directions to be taken and choices to be made.[32]

"Priestly obedience is lived in an atmosphere of constant readiness to allow oneself to be taken up, as it were "consumed," by the needs and demands of the flock, especially if they are truly reasonable and genuine."[33]

Being more conscious of, and informed about, their promise of obedience, priests are more likely to remember that they do not carry out their own ministry, but are fellow workers in helping the bishop carry out a common ministry. An expansive understanding of the promise of obedience is the only thing diocesan priests have in their arsenal that speaks directly to their unity as a group, because in it they promise each other to be "team players" with the bishop and with each other. This richer understanding of the promise of obedience will be essential in helping priests toward the renewal of their presbyterates.

The success of renewing presbyterates and their common sense of purpose rests primarily on enough bishops and priests wanting this unity. Priests need an honest dialogue that will help them recognize what to preserve from the past and what to embrace in the present and into the future. This honest dialogue could lead to developing a new paradigm with workable structures to enable them to offer better service to God's people and be better witnesses to the Gospel.

The church simply cannot afford to have infighting among its priests. Priests owe it to each other, to the next generation of priests and to the people they serve to become what the church says they are: "intimate sacramental brotherhoods" for a common ministry.

PARISH PRIEST AS SPIRITUAL LEADER

———— ಶ ————

PARISH PRIEST AS SPIRITUAL LEADER

Priests are teachers of the Word, ministers of the Sacraments and leaders of the Christian communities entrusted to them.

Lumen Gentium, no. 28[34]

The spirituality of a parish priest is, of course, rooted first of all in the spirituality of a baptized person, the daily living out of the death and resurrection of Christ. From there, this baptismal spirituality is lived out in the specific context of his ministry as a priest, just as married people live out their spirituality in the specific context of being marriage partners and parents. The Catechism says that these two sacraments are geared not merely to personal salvation, but toward the salvation of others. "…if they contribute as well to personal salvation, it is through service to others that they do so."[35] The spirituality of a marriage partner and a parish priest both come out of the context of "doing" their specific calls well.

At its most basic level, the spirituality of a priest is ecclesial; it is *for* the church. The parish priest is called from the laity, to live among the laity, to serve the mission and ministry of the laity. Here the parish priest has three functions: teacher of the Word, minister of the sacraments and leader of faith communities entrusted to him. The specific context of a parish priest's spirituality, then, is wrapped up in doing these three things well, just as a married person's spirituality is wrapped up in being a good spouse and good parent.

On the floor at the front door of Saint Meinrad Seminary is an inlaid school seal. Circling a few symbols are the words "*sanctitatae et scientia*," "holiness and knowledge," to remind future priests that they must be good *and* good at what they do. They must possess personal holiness *and* useful knowledge.

This idea is confirmed in Scripture in Jesus' teaching on the "Good Shepherd." Priests are called to act *in persona Christi*, and as such, the Good Shepherd is their model for ministry. There are at least two Greek words for "good," *agathos* and *kalos*. *Agathos* means "good," as in "morally good." *Kalos* means "good" as in "effective" or "good at" something. The "Good Shepherd" in the gospel is "*kalos*," "good at shepherding." Pope John Paul II, then, could be said to have been *agathos* and *kalos*, a good person who was good at shepherding. The spirituality of the parish priest involves being a good person **and** being a priest who is good at "priesting."

Neither personal holiness nor goodwill can replace competence. A priest today needs not only to be good and mean well, he needs to be good and good at what he does: he needs to be holy and competent. An emerging spirituality of the parish priest will be a matter not of one or the other, but of both. "Do not neglect the gift you have, which was conferred on you through the prophetic word with the imposition of hands of the presbyterate. Be diligent in these matters; be absorbed in them. Attend to yourself and your teaching, for by doing so you will save both yourself and those who listen to you" (I Timothy 4:14-16).

In the pre-Vatican II spirituality of parish priests, *agathos* was emphasized. It focused primarily on the ascetical and devotional aspects of the inner life. Celebrating the Eucharist, praying the breviary, saying the rosary, and engaging in other devotions were the source and fuel of their spirituality. Since Vatican Council II, we have seen a shift of emphasis that has added the *kalos*. This shift is more developmental than disjunctive, for it builds on the traditional staples of priestly spirituality. Priestly spirituality has evolved into an interdependence of *agathos* (a personally based spirituality) and *kalos* (a ministry based spirituality).

The emerging spirituality of a parish priest, therefore, can be thought of as a dialectical spirituality that is rooted in his life of faith and prayer and, at the same time, shaped and forged by the exercise of his ministerial priesthood. The former pole of the dialectic, personal holiness, is common to all the baptized. It is in the latter pole of the dialectic that we discover those things that allow us to speak of a spirituality proper to a diocesan priest. The spirituality unique to the parish priest is forged and shaped in his threefold role in the faith community: preacher, presider and leader, not **merely** in personal ascetical and devotional practices.

If a parish priest's spirituality is *ecclesial*, not merely *personal*, the priest is regarded as one who serves a *people-centered* community, a very different emphasis from that of a pre-Vatican II, *priest-centered* church. In a church understood as the people of God, the priest functions as a servant of God's people and as one whose ministry is exercised in cooperation with and interdependent upon other diverse ministries in the church. The spirituality of the parish priest, then, is forged and shaped by his threefold role in the faith community as teacher of the Word, minister of the celebration of the Sacraments and leader of the faith community. It is not enough for a parish priest to be personally *holy*; he must also be *good at* his three basic ministries.

Even though studies reveal that most parish priests enjoy the second of the three functions of priesthood, presider at the celebration of the sacraments, and some today would favor being "cultic" priests over "servant leader priests," we cannot be "cafeteria" priests, picking one and neglecting the other. We are called to be both at the same time.

Some parish priests have a call within a call. They are called to be pastors. The essential object of action as a pastor is the common good. As such, the pastor neesd to move from his own personal point of view to a viewing point. Unlike a seminarian or even an associate pastor, a pastor does not have the luxury of living merely in his personal point of view. Some never understand the difference, dividing congregations along "those who are with me and those who are against me." A pastor can never be the servant of an ideology or of a faction. A pastor always moves from a personal to a community dimension. It is his task, therefore, to reconcile differences of mentality in such a way that no one may feel himself a stranger in the community of the faithful. Pastors are defenders of the common good, with which they are charged in the name of the bishop. At the same time, they are strenuous defenders of the truth, lest the faithful be tossed about by every wind of opinion."[36]

When Jesus discussed leadership, it was always in terms of servanthood (cf. Mark 10:42-43). The servant image encourages us to view leadership not as power and prestige but as service and devotion. A servant model nowhere demands the abdication of the leadership role. Jesus was both servant and leader, and he never saw the two roles in a mutually exclusive way. Two extremes must be avoided: authoritarianism (exercising ministry in an overbearing manner) and abdication (disdaining the rightful role of leader). The key word here is *proper* authority. "The priest should avoid introducing into his pastoral ministry all forms of authoritarianism and forms of democratic administration which are alien to the profound reality of ministry, for these lead to secularization of the priest and a clericalization of the laity." [37]

A parish priest should never be part of any divisive group or destructive force. Some priests tend to align themselves, even beginning in the seminary, with sub-groups in their presbyterates and in the church in general, creating a destructive "them" and "us" climate of suspicion and even hate. This "virus" prevents people from engaging in respectful dialogue. It seems to have started in American politics a few years back and has now invaded our churches and even the hearts of some of its pastors.

How can a priest lead the community entrusted to his care to unity when he is part of the forces of disunity, even under the mantle of "orthodoxy?" In his encyclical, *Ecclesiam Suam,* Pope Paul VI said that our dialogue is "not proud; it is not bitter; it is not offensive; it is peaceful; it avoids violent methods and barbed words; it is patient; it is generous; it is respectful."[38]

There are two very different ways to herd sheep. One way is to walk in front of them, as the Good Shepherd himself did, gently calling to them while they follow behind, leading them where they need to go. The other way is to bark and snap from behind, like a sheep dog, chasing and intimidating them into going where they need to go. Good shepherds lead by invitation. Sheepdogs drive the sheep. Leaders pull. Bosses push.

Related to this is a tendency in public discourse these days to scold, and this tendency has invaded the words of some of the church's pastors. Father Bill Corcoran of Chicago has pointed out that many are worried about the effectiveness of the church when its leaders are perceived as the Village Scold. If pastors cannot approach their ministry in a positive way, then maybe it is best that they remain silent.

Parish priests are sometimes experienced by others as nabobs of negativity to all that society has to offer. Parish priests need to allow themselves to stand in awe of the good God has wrought in our world. They need to celebrate and give thanks for what is good about others, their mission, their vocation and their church. Dealing with error is necessary, but how one does it is also important. Parish priests need to remain on message, and that message is a Gospel of hope. When we lose hope, we scold. Spiritual leaders are dealers in hope, not in anger and pessimism.

More than a few veteran observers of the church insist that the most pressing need facing Catholicism today is the quality of its priestly leadership. No matter how one ranks the quality of priestly leadership on any scale of church priorities, it is clearly a matter of concern for the vitality of the church in whatever age the church finds itself.

The authenticity and maturity of the priest's spirituality remains the fundamental issue undergirding his preaching, presiding, facilitating and administering. Pastoral skills can be taught, but they remain techniques unless rooted in a mature spirituality, which often comes with age and experience. As younger and younger men are becoming pastors in the church, this maturity is becoming more and more important. Committing oneself to a high purpose does not mean one has necessarily developed the inner strength to carry through on that commitment.

In short, the spirituality of a parish priest involves integrating who a priest is with what a priest does, being a good person while being good at what a priest does, contributing to his own salvation through his service to others. If a parish priest is to be a "spiritual leader," he must claim his pulpit, claim his presider's chair and Sacramentary, and claim his position (and only his) as leader of the faith community.

CLAIMING YOUR PULPIT

Priest as Preacher of the Word

━━━━ ෨ ━━━━

CLAIMING YOUR PULPIT

Priest as Preacher of the Word

Priests have as their primary duty the proclamation of the gospel of God to all. For through the saving Word the spark of faith is struck in the hearts of unbelievers and fed in the hearts of the faithful.

Presbyterorum Ordinis, no. 4[39]

When it comes to spiritual leadership, the words of a famous Protestant preacher, Dwight Moody, may say it best. "The best way to revive a church is to build a fire in the pulpit." There is no better place for a priest to lead spiritually than from the pulpit, yet many parish priests squander this golden opportunity each and every week, either by being unprepared or by being trivial. If a priest has the burning desire to lead people spiritually, he must claim his pulpit.

Most people have heard of the term "bully pulpit," meaning a terrific platform from which to persuasively advocate an agenda. This term stems from President Theodore Roosevelt's reference to the White House as a "bully pulpit," a terrific platform from which to present his political ideas. Roosevelt often used the word "bully" as an adjective meaning "superb" or "wonderful."

A parish priest has a "bully pulpit," a terrific platform from which he can mold, form and lead the People of God. One can imagine how much the church would change for the better if priests would only claim their pulpits with passion. Catholic pulpits are indeed buried treasures waiting to be claimed. It is from there, mainly, that a priest can most effectively lead spiritually. Parish preaching could be defined as "group spiritual direction from the pulpit."

The pastor, most of all, must claim his pulpit by committing himself personally to dynamic preaching as well as to overseeing and planning the preaching ministry of the parish. It is his job to work closely with and guide associate pastors, deacons, indeed anyone who is charged with the ministry of preaching, with a deliberate and coherent plan of action. It is the pastor's role to ask, "Where do we want to lead this congregation, and what do we do to get there?"

Saint Gregory the Great has some interesting things to say about preaching in his treatise, "Pastoral Care." He says that the preacher should be both profitable in speech and discreet in keeping silence, lest he keep secret what should be uttered and utter what should be kept secret. Often, he says, priests, being afraid of losing human favor, fear to speak freely of what is right, being what Isaiah 56:10 calls "dumb dogs, unable to bark." On the others hand, he says, when the spiritual leader prepares to speak, he must bear in mind to exercise a studious caution in his speech, for if his discourse, hastily given, be ill-ordered, the hearts of his hearers may be stricken with the wound of error, and when he wishes to appear wise, he will by his lack of wisdom sever the bonds of unity. [40]

Saint Gregory the Great also addresses the issue of talking too much. Often, he says, the force of what is said is enfeebled in the hearts of the hearers by a careless and offensive torrent of words.[41] At a priest retreat, Father Walter Burghardt called such preaching constipation of thought and diarrhea of the mouth.

If the primary duty of priests is to proclaim the gospel, then "much will be required of the person entrusted with much" (Luke 12:48). Failing to appreciate the power of the Word and squandering the "bully pulpits" entrusted to them has to be among the biggest sins parish priests can commit.

If the "primary duty" of priests is to preach, then it's easier said than done! Even though Vatican Council II made this decree in 1965, ask any honest Catholic 42 years later and they will tell you that priests are still failing in their "primary duty." Catholics are crossing parish and diocesan boundaries looking for solid spiritual food and when they fail to find it, they leave us to join those independent mega churches that are springing up all over the country and sucking people out of our parishes at an alarming rate. It's past time to translate "the primary duty of the priest is to preach" from wishful thinking to an obvious reality! Before one can become a "preaching specialist" for the church, several things must be considered.

THE PURPOSE OF PREACHING

The purpose of preaching is "...to summon all men urgently to conversion and to holiness."[42] A parish priest cannot summon others to conversion and holiness without having been converted to holiness himself. Otherwise he may become another kind of "preaching specialist," a clever manipulator of people for his own ends, but he will not be a "priest," a medium of God's "good news." He may be able to entertain, make people laugh or cry or give him their money, but he will never be able to lead them to conversion and to holiness without being converted and holy himself.

PREACH WHAT?

"Parish priests are not called to preach their own wisdom but God's Word."[43] They are called to preach the "gospel." The word gospel means "good news." The first question a serious homilist must ask himself is, "Can I describe in a few words what the "good news" is that Jesus came to bring to the world and I am commissioned to announce?" If not, he should stay clear of pulpits until he can! Sadly enough, there are priests and deacons who have been "preaching" for years and seminarians about to be ordained after five or six years in the seminary who cannot answer that question.

The "good news" is, and the bottom line of every homily should be, this: God loves us without condition, no ands, ifs or buts about it!" It's the message of the Covenant. It's the message of the parables. It's the message of the Passion, Death and Resurrection of Jesus. When a preacher himself does not understand or believe this "good news," he usually ends up preaching an opposing message of conditional love.

Parish priests are called to preach the "gospel," not their own opinions, prejudices, pet peeves or wisdom. If their trips to Europe do not help enlighten the gospel text, then they shouldn't be brought up! Besides, it is insensitive at best not to think about all those families in front of us who will never be able to afford such trips. Regardless of how funny his latest joke is, if it doesn't enlighten what Jesus had to say, he needs to save it for another occasion. Serious preachers are not called to do stand-up comedy from the pulpit. Nor is preaching a scripture class or a theology lecture. People are not interested in where the preacher went on vacation, how funny he is, what he is angry about or how much he knows. Preaching is not about the preacher, but about helping people respond to Christ's invitation to discipleship. Priests are the earthenware jar, not the treasure!

"...all preaching of the church must be nourished and ruled by sacred Scripture. For in the sacred books, the Father who is in heaven meets His children with great love and speaks with them; and the force and power in the word of God is so great that it remains the support and energy of the church, the strength and faith of her sons [and daughters], the food of the soul, the pure and perennial source of spiritual life."[44]

"Appropriate use must be made not only of theological principles, but also of the findings of the secular sciences, especially psychology and sociology. Thus the faithful can be brought to live the faith in a more thorough and mature way."[45]

The priest is to be a bridge builder who links the human and the divine. To do so effectively, he must know the terrain on both ends of the bridge, as well as the bridge itself. One of the most infamous examples of the preacher not knowing himself is the preacher who has not dealt with his own sexuality, who has not integrated his own sexual energy. He will be a preacher obsessed, not with the "good news," but with sex, sexual morality and other people's sex lives, as a substitute for dealing with his own sexual issues. This will be done, of course, under the cover of "promoting morality." The key here is the word "obsessed."

A PASSION FOR PREACHING

"The priest himself ought first of all to develop a great personal familiarity with the word of God. He needs to approach the word with a docile and prayerful heart so that it may deeply penetrate his thoughts and feelings and bring about a new outlook in him — "the mind of Christ." Only if he "abides" in the Word will the priest become a perfect disciple of the Lord. The priest ought to be the first "believer" in the word." [46]

The priest is able to proclaim the word of God only to the extent that that word has burned into his heart and is lived in his life. Before one can be a Samuel, "not permitting any word of his to be without effect" (I Samuel 3:19), he must be a Jeremiah for whom preaching became "like a fire burning in my heart, imprisoned in my bones; I grow weary holding it in" (Jeremiah 20:9), and "When I found your words, I devoured them; they became my joy and the happiness of my heart (Jeremiah 15:16). "For from the fullness of the heart the mouth speaks" (Luke 6:45). "*Nemo dat quod non habet.*" "If you don't have it, you cannot give it!" (Old Latin Maxim). "If the story is in you, it has got to come out" (William Faulkner).

Serious preaching is not for cowards and the faint of heart. Only one who is on a serious, personal, spiritual quest can ever become an effective "preaching specialist." The "preaching specialist" must know the word of God, know people and know himself, more than the average preacher! A "preaching specialist's" main tools are the Scriptures, the newspaper and his own spiritual journals.

FOCUSED ATTENTION

No one is born a "preaching specialist." It starts with a dream. It is nourished by faith. It is perfected by focused attention.

"Those who believe they can and those who believe they can't are both right" (Henry Ford). The priest who really believes that he can become a "preaching specialist" will commit to it, but results will not come cheaply. This kind of skill takes years of focused attention. Translating such a dream into reality takes great courage. Doubt is a constant enemy. When doubt reigns, there is a strong temptation to let go of part of the dream as a way of resolving inevitable tensions. Success depends on the ability to remain enthusiastic, focused and purposeful to the end. "For the vision still has its time, presses on to fulfillment and will not disappoint. If it delays, wait for it. It will surely come. It will not be late" (Habakkuk 2:3). "When the student is ready, the teacher will appear!" "God loves to help him who strives to help himself" (Aeschylus, Fragment 223).

ORGANIZED FOR SUCCESS

"For want of a nail the shoe is lost, for want of a shoe the horse is lost, for want of a horse the rider is lost."[47] Every dream benefits by a good plan. Every would-be "preaching specialist" must develop his own "personal homiletics resource center:" a comfortable place to think and work, a computer program for the storing and retrieval of one's work, a library of commentaries, familiar quotations, a biblical thesaurus as well as a regular thesaurus, a paper filing system for clippings and ideas, a handheld tape recorder with blank tapes, and a journal of personal experiences.

A serious preacher asks people for feedback. He could end up with several boxes of letters from people from whom he has solicited affirmations, ideas and constructive criticisms. He will find that when he feeds them, they in turn will feed him, setting up a cycle of energy that gives him the courage and determination to keep preaching. Their responses are what make it all worth it. There is something magic in helping people get in touch with God.

Roman Catholics are starving for good preaching. They are moving from parish to parish looking for it. When they don't find it within our church, they now feel free to leave and look for it in other places, like the independent Christian churches springing up all across the country. This is not as much about their strength nearly as much as it is about our weakness. Parishioners do not leave their parishes over what is happening on our altars, but for what is not happening in our pulpits. However, because of what is not happening in our pulpits, people probably do not understand what is happening on our altars.

Catholics may be angry that preaching is restricted to the ordained mainly because priests are doing such a poor job. If you're going to hog the pulpit, you need to be able to bring home the bacon!

A HOMILY, NOT A SERMON[48]

It might be a good idea to end these words about preaching by offering a simple template for a good homily. This simple template will hopefully offer a simple way to produce the multiple weekly homilies required of parish priests today.

It was Origen (185-253) who first distinguished between *logos* (or *sermo*) and *homilia* (or *tractatus*). *Logos* followed the intricate shape of classical rhetoric, while the form of *homilia* was direct and free. *Homilia* was a popular exposition *and* application of scripture.

Just as Origen made a distinction between *logos* and *homilia*, the reformers of Vatican II wanted to distinguish the homily from the popular form of preaching of the day, the sermon. While the sermon often relied on biblical texts, especially to prove a doctrinal point, it is not necessarily rooted in the scriptural texts of the day.

Before Vatican II, the sermon was referred to as a "secondary interruption" of the liturgy. In the post-conciliar church, the homily is seen as "flowing from the sacred text" and a "highly esteemed as part of the liturgy itself."

Four characteristics of preaching were restored from Origen's ancient tradition by Vatican II in order to distinguish this renewed form of preaching, the homily, from other forms, especially a sermon. Homiletic preaching is (a) biblical, (b) liturgical, (c) kerygmatic, and (d) familiar.

A SIMPLE TEMPLATE FOR A GOOD HOMILY

Crafting a simple homily can be a three-step process: the introduction, the body and the application. Rather than beginning with the introduction, one can go directly to the body, then to the introduction and finally the application.

STEP ONE: Writing a homily always begins with the Scriptures. It is important to look at why the church has chosen to put these readings together, as well as to look at each reading individually. It might be a good idea to read and re-read all the scriptures of the day several times, looking for a thread that runs through all of them, but also for a significant point in one of them, usually the gospel. This is a lot like running a metal detector over the whole field. Once there seems to be a "click," an idea or concept that could be developed, dig there. It is important to find one idea to develop, rather than trying to "unload the whole load of hay." This is especially true if one wants to develop a coherent, memorable, understandable and useful idea in a twelve-minute homily. Once an idea is "mined" from the text and researched, you are ready to go to step two, the introduction.

STEP TWO: Once a nugget has been mined from Scriptures, look for a similar insight in real life (story, movie, book, personal experience or the news) that makes a point similar to the one in Scripture. That way one can move the congregation from the familiar to the new.

A joke that has nothing to do with the point of the homily, just to loosen up the crowd, should be avoided. Comedy in homiletics should be used sparingly in general. This holds true of priests telling people about their vacation or trip to Europe or the Holy Land, unless it clearly enlightens the point one hopes to make from the Scriptures. (A vacation story to a church full of families who cannot afford to take a vacation can actually distance one from one's audience.)

As much as possible, a story or reference should have some universal appeal. People in the congregation should be able to say to themselves, "Yes, I have had a similar experience!" The most basic rule, therefore, should be to help them grasp what the scripture is saying by comparing it to a real-life situation today. Jesus did this in his parables. He compared something they knew with something they did not know so that they could be brought to an "ah-ha" experience.

STEP THREE: The final step is to apply this new insight to their lives and yours. A liberal use of the word "we," rather than "you people," is preferable. Father Damien, the leper, saw his homilies improve radically the day he was able to say, "We lepers." In short, this part of the homily seeks to show ways that we can all apply the insight of the day's Scriptures to our own lives.

As with Origen, the *homilia* or homily is not a scripture class, not a theology lecture, not an opportunity to push one's personal pet peeves or to lambaste the congregation, nor is it a time to promote the latest parish/diocesan program. It is a *popular exposition of scripture.* It is meant to be *free and direct.* Besides being biblically based, it is also meant to fit well into the whole liturgy of the day, be an exposition of the basic teaching of Jesus, and to be easily understandable and useful to ordinary people.

It takes a wise person, one who can bring together knowledge and practical experience, to prepare a good homily. If only theologians can understand the preacher's message, the priest may be "smart" but not necessarily "wise." If a preacher is not smart enough, and in touch enough with the non-elite, to communicate his knowledge to them, then that preacher should probably not be giving homilies in parishes. The purpose of a homily is not to impress nor judge the listener, but to engage and encourage the listener in serious discipleship.

The spiritual leadership of a parish priest requires that he take his role as preacher with the greatest of seriousness by becoming a "preaching specialist." The parish pulpit is certainly the primary place for such spiritual leadership. The parish priest, who would be a serious spiritual leader, needs to claim his pulpit.

As a sacred place like the altar itself, the best place to give a homily is *from the pulpit.* Just as walking up and down the aisles with plate and cup in hand, consecrating the sacred species, would lessen the sacredness of that act, preaching outside the pulpit, in many instances, seems to lessen the sacredness of the preached word.

There are a lot of strong feelings about whether to write out, or not to write out, homilies. To be a serious spiritual leader in a busy parish it might be a wise idea, especially if one has worked long and hard on a homily, to write it out and save it so as to get as much mileage out of it as possible.

1. Printed homilies give preachers the advantage of using the right turn of phrase, avoiding repetition and using words economically. The objections of "sounding like it's being read" can be overcome by developing a writing style for speaking, which is very different from an ordinary writing style meant for reading. Even if the text is only glanced at in the pulpit, the discipline of writing it out will keep the preacher from rambling, repeating himself and searching for the right word while on his feet and from memory.

2. Printed homilies offer a way to connect the praying community with those who cannot physically be there because of sickness or various other reasons. If the parish priest wants to spiritually guide the whole congregation,

and not just those who show up on weekends, he could share his preaching in various other ways — printed or recorded.

3. While re-using homilies may be a bad idea generally speaking, saved homilies can be adapted in a squeeze, especially when one does multiple weddings and funerals of unfamiliar people or when unforeseen parish events unexpectedly encroach on the priest's valuable time. Saved homilies, when filed well, can be retrieved and organized around themes for days of recollection, parish missions and retreats, or even turned into spiritual reading books. Assuming that a parish priest works hard to preach, why not squeeze as much juice out of his work as possible by saving it in text form?

In short, having a library of well-crafted, smartly filed and easily retrieved homilies may be one of the smartest ways for parish priests, as spiritual leaders, to use their valuable time well. It beats starting from scratch or "winging it" every time they are called on to preach. The discipline of writing is also itself a spiritual exercise for the one doing the writing.

CLAIMING YOUR RITUAL BOOKS

Priest as Minister
of the Sacraments

—————— ⅋⊃ ——————

CLAIMING YOUR RITUAL BOOKS

Priest as Minister of the Sacraments

Pastors of souls must realize that, when the liturgy is celebrated, more is required than the mere observance of the laws governing valid and licit celebration. It is their duty also to ensure that the faithful take part knowingly, actively, and fruitfully.

Sacrosanctum Concilium, no. 11[49]

Preaching Scripture and celebrating Sacraments are one and the same: proclamation of Good News. Both are invitations seeking a response. In the Vatican II church, at long last, we can do both together. Younger priests may not realize that one of the greatest contributions of the Second Vatican Council was the giving of the Holy Scriptures to the laity in general, as well as broader use of it in the celebration of the sacraments in particular.

The sacraments, privileged moments in communicating the divine life to people, are at the very heart of priestly ministry. When priests celebrate the sacraments, they act *in the person* of Christ.

As such, two things are required.

1. Even though Christ can act through flawed human beings, if one is to act in the person of Christ, a credible lifestyle is a must. St. Augustine says, "Christ's gift is not profaned by a weak minister; what flows through him

keeps its purity, and what passes through him remains. What passes through defiled human beings is not itself defiled."[50] Even though the message does not depend on the goodness of the messenger, a priest should mold his life in such a way that he becomes a bridge and not an obstacle.

2. A high standard of ceremony and liturgical celebration, free from spectacle and personal taste for styles foreign to the community, is required. The best dictum may be, "Do what is in the book, with its approved options, well."

The core of priestly ministry is the celebration of the Eucharist, within which the Word plays a significant part, "the source and summit"[51] of the Christian life. Baptism, Confirmation and Eucharist are sacraments of initiation. Reconciliation and the Anointing of the Sick are sacraments of healing. The celebration of Orders by bishops and the celebration of Marriage, witnessed by priests and deacons, are sacraments of service.

Parish priests, to be effective spiritual leaders, need not only to have a great personal familiarity with the Word of God, but also a great personal familiarity with the liturgical texts of the church. He should be able to handle them with care and navigate them with ease so as to unleash their power to transform the lives of those who celebrate the Sacraments.

How many times have we seen priests, during the celebration of one of the Sacraments, flipping through the rituals, looking for a "good" option, only to settle for "anything will do?"

How many times have we seen priests, during the celebration of one of the Sacraments, handling the ritual as if it were a cookbook instead of a love letter? There is a difference between "hitting the keys" and "making music."

How many times have we seen priests, during the celebration of one of the Sacraments, handle the ritual as if he is "doing his own thing," rather than presiding over the integration of other ministries of music and readings, as well as the handling of sacred objects and the graceful use of sacred space? More is required than reading the words of the rituals correctly.

A parish priest who wants to be an effective spiritual leader needs to use the rituals of the church in such a way that people "connect" to God. He needs to be able to handle not only rituals, but also pulpits, altars, presidential chairs, baptismal fonts, bread and wine, water and oil, vessels and vesture with ease and class. He needs to recognize the rituals and sacramentals that he handles as tools for effective spiritual leadership.

If the whole point of liturgy is to intensify the daily growth of Catholics in Christian living, should not a parish priest handle his "tools" with the greatest care so as to unleash maximum benefit in the lives of those he serves?

"Pastors of souls must therefore realize that when the liturgy is celebrated, more is required than the mere observance of the laws governing valid and licit celebration. It is their duty also to ensure that the faithful take part knowingly, actively and fruitfully."[52]

"Yet it would be futile to entertain any hopes of realizing this goal unless the pastors themselves, to begin with, become thoroughly penetrated with the spirit and power of the liturgy and become masters of it. It is vitally necessary, therefore, that attention be directed, above all, to the liturgical instruction of the clergy."[53]

Being a validly ordained priest is not enough, in itself, for adequate spiritual leadership. Priests are called, as well, to "take care to cultivate an appropriate knowledge and facility in the liturgy, so that by their own liturgical ministry, the Christian communities entrusted to them may more and more adequately give praise to God."[54]

When a spiritual leader understands and uses his ritual books well, he can say with the Psalmist, "Those times I recall as I pour out my soul, when I went in procession with the crowd, I went with them to the house of God, amid loud cries of thanksgiving, with the multitude keeping festival" (Psalm 42:5).

CLAIMING YOUR AUTHORITY

Priest as Leader in the Community

———— ℰ℧ ————

CLAIMING YOUR AUTHORITY

Priest as Leader in the Community

Indeed, the ministerial priesthood does not of itself signify a greater degree of holiness with regard to the common priesthood of the faithful; through it Christ gives to priests, in the Spirit, a particular gift so that he can help the People of God to exercise faithfully and fully the common priesthood which it has received.

Pastores Dabo Vobis, no. 17[55]

Before a priest can claim his place as leader of the Christian community, he needs to know his place. He needs to claim his position, yes, but only his position.

In a church understood as the People of God, the priest functions as a servant of God's people and as one whose ministry is exercised in cooperation with and interdependent upon other diverse ministries in the church. The first two canons of individual pastoral care are (a) knowledge of the people and friendly relations with them, and (b) the harmonizing of personal pastoral care with a community vision of pastoral ministry.

With that said, a parish priest is nonetheless an important leader in the community entrusted to him. "Moved by pastoral charity he should not fear to exercise proper authority in those areas where he is obliged to exercise it, for he has been constituted in authority for this very purpose. Today "authority" has a bad name, but when authority is duly exercised it is done not so much to command as to serve. Parish priests must overcome the temptation to exempt themselves from this responsibility. If they do not exercise authority, they no longer serve."[56]

Authority can be abused in at least two ways: too much and too little. "The priest should avoid introducing into his pastoral ministry all forms of authoritarianism and forms of democratic administration which are alien to the profound reality of ministry, for these lead to a secularization of the priest and a clericalization of the laity."[57]

In their pastoral ministry, parish priests share in the ministry of their bishops. Priests make the bishop present in the individual local congregations entrusted to them. As trusted co-workers of the bishop, priests do not carry out their own ministry, but help the bishop carry out his ministry.

The essential object of a pastor's ministry is to be a defender of the common good. As such, he never becomes a servant of an ideology or of a faction. The pastor always moves from a personal point of view to a viewing point. It is his task to reconcile differences of mentality in such a way that no one may feel himself a stranger in the community of the faithful. At the same time, pastors are strenuous defenders of the truth, lest the faithful be tossed about by every wind of opinion.[58]

Parochial vicars share in the ministry of a pastor. Parochial vicars are co-workers with the pastor in common counsel and endeavor with him and also under his authority. A parochial vicar can be assigned to assist in fulfilling the entire pastoral ministry on behalf of the entire parish, a definite part of the parish, or a certain group of the Christian faithful of the parish; he can be assigned to assist in fulfilling a certain type of ministry in different parishes concurrently.[59]

Priests are not priests simply one by one. They serve the church in a presbyterate in union with the bishop. As trusted co-workers of the bishop, priests relate to each other not as "lone rangers" or individuals in "private practice," but as an "intimate sacramental brotherhood"[60] for service. The Sacrament of Holy Orders is conferred upon each of them as individuals, but they are inserted into the communion of the presbyterate united with the bishop. This sacramental brotherhood implies that each member is bound to the others through a sense of common purpose and a sense of collaboration in diocesan mission. They serve as the bishop's unified ministry team in order to offer coherent and unified ministry to the People of God.

The diaconate and the presbyterate are graded participations in the bishop's ministry. Contrary to common wisdom, the diaconate is not a subordination to the presbyterate, but one of the two ministerial arms of the bishop. The deacon is not an "almost priest," nor is he one who fills in the gaps where priests are not available. Deacons are ministers of service. As ministers of service, they are charged with promoting the *diaconia* of the whole church. They do not serve *for* the church, but rather inspire, motivate and train others for service. Priests and deacons are subordinate to the bishop directly, each with their own unique ministries.

In conclusion, if a parish priest is to be an effective spiritual leader, he will know his place and claim his place, but only his place. Pope John Paul II lays out quite well in *Pastores Dabo Vobis* the relationship of a priest to the People of God. "Through the ministerial priesthood, Christ gives to priests in the Spirit, a particular gift so that they can help the people of God exercise faithfully the common priesthood which it has received." He also says, "The priesthood is not an institution that exists alongside the laity, or "above" it. The priesthood is "for" the laity; precisely for this reason it possess a ministerial character, that is to say, one "of service."[61]

Vatican Council II[62] said, "Priests must sincerely acknowledge and promote the dignity of the laity and the role which is proper to them in the mission of the church." Priests do not take over the place of the laity; they help the laity take their own rightful place in the church.

With that said, claiming one's place is much more complicated than claiming one's title. One does not become a spiritual leader by merely filling an office, wearing a robe, taking course work in the subject or even resolving in one's own will to do this task. The proof of spiritual leadership is in the results, not simply in holding an office or title.

WHERE ARE YOU
and
WHERE ARE THEY?

——————— ༄ ———————

WHERE ARE YOU and WHERE ARE THEY?

You can only lead people if you are at least one step ahead of those you lead.

Dr. M. Scott Peck

The first order of business when one is called to spiritual leadership is to assess clearly the stage of one's own spirituality. This is essential before trying to lead anyone else spiritually.

The second order of business is to assess clearly the stages of spirituality of the people he is attempting to lead. This is essential before trying to lead them somewhere else.

One chapter in Dr. M. Scott Peck's 1987 book, *The Different Drum*,[63] helped me more than anything else to understand this essential step in spiritual leadership. His insights are based on James Fowler's 1982 *Stages of Faith*.[64] Dr. Peck has made the concept of spiritual growth simple and attractive to a generation of spiritual seekers operating inside and outside church structures.

Dr. Peck presents, in a very popular way, the *esoteric* side of religion to a generation who has given up on the *exoteric* side of religion. The *exoteric* is focused on the structures, rules and forms of formal religion. The *esoteric* is focused on what happens *inside* a person. Dr. Peck calls the *esoteric* side of religion *spirituality*.

Dr. Peck's weakness is not that he is a "populist," but that he is part of a trend that separates *spirituality* from *religion*. In this trend, *spirituality* is understood as good, while *religion* is understood as bad.

Organized religion, of course, has brought this upon itself. The sterility of organized religion gave birth to this divorce by not being able to satisfy a growing ravenous appetite for spiritual growth, mainly because it was too focused on preserving religion's *exoteric* side. The ideal is when both the *esoteric* and *exoteric* sides of religion are in balance — when religion has a heart, when God is experienced in the structures, rules and forms of formal religion.

One can learn from multiple sources. The truth is the truth, no matter who speaks it. One can learn something very important, even from the likes of Dr. M. Scott Peck. He argues that just as there are discernible stages in human physical and psychological growth, there are also stages in human spiritual growth.

Dr. Peck's summary of these stages can be useful in helping spiritual leaders understand where they are coming from personally and where other people with different religious perspectives and styles are coming from as well.

His insights can help priests understand why certain people are attracted to certain parishes, why people have such strong reactions to change, why people think the way they think and even why certain people choose to leave the church altogether. His insights can help pastors, especially, understand how important it is to honor a gamut of styles of spirituality in order to hold as many of these people as possible together in one community. His insights can help spiritual leaders become more inclusive and less exclusive by realizing that people can be at different places on the same path.

STAGE I: UNDEVELOPED SPIRITUALITY

Most young children and perhaps one in five adults fall into Stage I. It is essentially a stage of undeveloped spirituality.

It is called "antisocial" because those adults who are in it seem generally incapable of loving others. Their relationships with their fellow human beings are essentially manipulative and self-serving. They really don't give a hoot about anyone else's needs or rights.

It is called "chaotic" because these people are basically un-principled. Being unprincipled, there is nothing that governs them except their own will. Since their will from moment to moment can go this way or that, there is a lack of integrity to their being. They often end up in jail or find themselves in various forms of social difficulty. They may be quite disciplined in getting what they want, so they may rise to positions of considerable prestige and power, even corporate presidents or influential preachers. Usually these people go through their whole life this way and ride it out unchanged. Some may even kill themselves, unable to envision change.

Some, however, will convert to Stage II. These conversions are usually sudden and dramatic. They get to the point that anything is preferable to the chaos. They are willing to do anything to liberate themselves from the chaos, even to the point of submitting themselves to an institution for their governance. They become model prisoners. They may join the military or some other tightly structured organization, like a fundamentalist or highly organized church.

STAGE II: INSTITUTIONAL SPIRITUALITY

Several things characterize the behavior of men and women in stage II, which is the stage of a majority of churchgoers.

One characteristic of people in this stage is their attachment to the forms of religion, which is why it is called "institutional." They are so attached to religious forms that they become very upset if changes are made to the words or the music or in the traditional order of things. Since it was precisely these forms that were responsible for their liberation from chaos, it is no wonder that people at this stage of spiritual development become so threatened when someone seems to be "messing" with the rules. The more torn up people are inside, the more they need externals to anchor them. This is precisely why they are in stage II. These structures are what give their lives order.

A second characteristic of people in this stage is their perception of God. People in stage II tend to envision God almost entirely as that of an external, transcendent Being. They have little understanding of an immanent, indwelling God. But once again, it is no accident that their vision of God is that of a giant benevolent Cop in the Sky, because that is precisely the kind of God they need.

A third characteristic of people in this stage is the high value they place on stability. Children raised in this stability absorb the principles of their parents until the day comes, usually in late adolescence, when they want to be free of such stability. They want to be self-governing human beings. They begin converting, to the chagrin of their parents, to stage III. They become skeptical individuals. They often call themselves "agnostics."

STAGE III: INDIVIDUALISTIC SPIRITUALITY

These so-called "nonbelievers" are often more spiritually developed than many who are content to remain in stage II. Although individualistic, they are not the least bit anti-social. To the contrary, they are often deeply committed and involved in social causes. They make up their own minds about things. They don't believe everything they hear, even from the church. They often make loving and intensely dedicated parents.

Advanced stage III people are active truth seekers. If people in stage III seek truth deeply and widely enough, they find what they are looking for, but they never find all the pieces of the puzzle. Yet they are able to get a glimpse of the whole picture and see that it is indeed beautiful and resembles those "primitive myths" and "superstitions" that their parents and grandparents believed in. At this point they can begin their conversion to stage IV, which is the mystic and communal stage of spiritual development.

STAGE IV: MYSTICAL SPIRITUALITY

Mystics are people who can see the underlying connectedness of all things. They realize that we are all integral parts of the same unity. Mystics acknowledge the enormity of the unknown. Rather than being frightened by it, they seek to penetrate it, realizing that the deeper they go, the greater the mystery will become. In dramatic contrast to those in stage II who need simple, clear-cut dogmatic structures and have little taste for the unknown and unknowable, those in stage IV embrace mystery. People in stage IV enter religion to approach mystery. Stage II people enter religion to escape mystery.

Stage IV people are most aware that the whole world is a community and that what divides us into warring camps is precisely the lack of this awareness. When stage IV people re-enter religion, they return with new eyes. They do not need answers for everything. They are often quite ecumenical. They often do more than the law requires.

SOME CONCLUSIONS

There are, of course, many gradations within and between the four stages of spiritual development.

People between Stage I and II are often called "backsliders." These are the people who, for example, get "saved" in a fundamentalist church from a dissolute life of drinking and gambling, only to fall back into it after a year or two of living a sober, God-fearing life. They may need to be "saved" a second time and often continue to bounce back and forth between stage I and stage II.

Likewise, people bounce back and forth between stages II and III. These are the Catholics, for example, who leave the church, only to be eaten up by guilt. They may "try it again" by going to Midnight Mass or by making Lenten resolutions to return to the church, only to find out they are unable to maintain those commitments. It is not that they did not have good intentions in trying, but that they often find that "their heads are not there" anymore.

These Catholics may not realize that there is another place to go except to go back. They don't know that they can to go forward. Stage IV gives them the option of coming back to the church but with a different set of eyes, with a more adult faith.

Similarly, people bounce back and forth between stage III and stage IV. People in stage III often become intrigued by the spiritual things that stage IV has to offer, but it scares them and they return to the "rational" safety of stage III. They fear being caught up in something that they may not be able to manage and, even worse, they fear they may like it. This is especially true of people who have been hurt when they were in stage II. They fear being hurt again if they get involved in religion again. They are tempted and fearful at the same time.

There also exists a sense of threat among people in the different stages of spiritual development, and it is necessary for parish priests and parish staffs to deal constructively with these perceived threats.

Those in stage I, adopting a pretense of being "cool" and "having it altogether," are threatened by just about everything and everybody. People in stage II are not threatened by the "sinners" in stage I. They are actually seen as a goldmine of converts.

Those in stage II may be very threatened by the skeptics of stage III and even more by the mystics of stage IV, who believe in many of the same things they believe in, but with a freedom they find absolutely terrifying.

Stage III people are neither threatened by people in stage I (whom they regard as unprincipled) nor stage II (whom they regard as superstitious), but they are cowed by stage IV people who seem to be very much like themselves, yet somehow still believe some of the crazy "God stuff" that people in stage II believe.

It is extremely important for parish priests, especially pastors, to be cognizant of these threats. They can only lead other people if they are at least one step ahead of them. If they are too far ahead, they will likely lose them. If they are too far behind them, they may not know how to reach them and may even consider them evil.

An understanding of the stages is important for building community. A group of parishioners, all in one stage of spirituality, is not so much a community as it is a clique. A true community will likely include people of all ages and stages.

Care, however, needs to be taken to deal constructively with the threats between people of different stages. When spiritual leaders cannot embrace a variety of spiritualities, they end up running parishes that specialize in their own stage of spirituality. We see these "specialty" parishes developing in every diocese. People gravitate toward those who honor them and away from those who reject them.

Conversions between stages I and II are usually sudden and dramatic, while conversions between stage II and IV are generally gradual. It is during the process of conversion from stage II to stage IV that people generally become conscious that there is such a thing as spiritual growth. These conversions are not so much directed by spiritual leaders as much as by God himself. It is then a matter of honoring them by allowing God to direct them.

The challenge for parish priests who want to be effective spiritual leaders, especially in today's church, is to find a way to facilitate the conversion between those who are ready to move from stage II to stage IV without them having to spend a whole adult life in stage III. Even so, spiritual leaders could benefit by remembering that arriving at stage IV is just the beginning of a lifelong process from which no one graduates.

HOW DOES
SPIRITUAL GROWTH
HAPPEN?

———— ⽈ ————

HOW DOES SPIRITUAL GROWTH HAPPEN?

I planted, Apollos watered, but God caused the growth.

I Corinthians 3:6

The assumption in this section is that "spirituality" is about the personal, internal change and growth that leads to deeper discipleship, not merely about the multiplication of religious rituals, pious practices or parish involvements, no matter how helpful they may be in the process of transformation. In fact, when one cannot inspire and lead spiritually, there is a temptation to hide behind a merely cultic role as a priest and the activism of parish life.

Just as God calls and gradually makes leaders out of those who answer his call, God makes spiritual growth happen *within* those who answer his call to discipleship. Conversion may happen in an instant, but spiritual growth and transformation may require years. If priests are to be midwives in this process, then they need to understand how spiritual growth happens.

The best scriptural story to explain how spiritual growth happens may just be the story of the Exodus. Exodus is the story of people being called to something new, setting out in excitement, being tempted in discouragement to back out of the process, the decision for fidelity and finally arriving at a new level of growth.

In this section of the book, on how spiritual growth happens, I offer a series of talks, entitled "Taking Charge of Your Own Spiritual Transformation," that I gave to the Cathedral of the Assumption congregation in Louisville, Kentucky, during my (1983-1997) tenure. After preaching God's call to "conversion" for several years, the congregation began to complain, "We hear you! We have answered the call! Now tell us where to go from here!" Conversion is, of course, God's gift, but transformation is the result of people's grace-filled responses to their calls to holiness and deeper discipleship.

These contain the spiritual concepts and Scriptural themes that guided me in my role as "spiritual leader" for that congregation. God called them to holiness and gave them the ability to respond, but I was Moses, so to speak, inviting them to accept God's invitation and prodding them to stay the course, knowing, as Pope John Paul II put it, that "All formation is ultimately self-formation."

TAKING CHARGE OF YOUR OWN SPIRITUAL TRANSFORMATION

"When Opportunity Comes Knocking"

Given on February 28, 1993

Jesus was led into the desert by the Spirit
to be tempted by the devil.

Matthew 4:1

THE most significant event of my life, even more significant than being ordained, happened in the spring of 1965. I was extremely bashful. I avoided meeting new people or getting myself into unfamiliar situations. I was scared of life. I was what George Bernard Shaw called a feverish little clod of grievances and ailments, complaining that the world would not dedicate itself to making me happy.

That day, I was standing on a fire escape outside my room at Saint Meinrad Seminary with a fellow seminarian, Pat Murphy. In what had to be a moment of grace, an impulse gift from God, I suddenly blurted out, "Pat, I am so sick and tired of being bashful and scared of life that I'm going to do something about it even if it kills me!"

I was shocked by the words that came out of my own mouth! But from that moment on, I have been standing up to the coward in me. I have been deliberately "slaying dragons" and "confronting demons," in my head and on my path, ever since. I would not be where I am today if that "moment of grace" had not happened and if I had not responded enthusiastically. I decided that day not to indulge my resistance to personal and spiritual growth anymore. That day, on that fire escape, I made my first conscious decision to enter the world of spiritual growth and deliberate living. How appropriate and symbolic that the decision was made on a "fire escape!" Up to that point, my life had been guided by the belief that "life is something that happens to you and all you can do is make the most of it."

That day, on that fire escape, I finally learned a fundamental principle of spiritual growth: Fear and pain cannot be used as excuses for backing off from life. From that day on, I have come to understand that pain serves a purpose. Pain captures our attention and lets us know that change is necessary. Pain signals that it is time to move on and learn new behaviors. Unfortunately, many of us sabotage the possibility of growth by denying, numbing or backing away from pain. We live in a culture that incessantly tells us that pain is to be avoided at all costs! This is where "following the crowd" is deadly, for there is no spiritual and personal health without embracing good pain. The wise know when pain must be embraced. Fools run from any hint of it!

Jesus embraced a much greater eye-opening experience at his baptism. In his moment of grace, Jesus realized where he was being called, who was calling him and why he needed to commit himself to the path that would take him there.

His "desert experience" was actually a preview of what lay ahead — demons! We need not be too literal here. "Demons" can be those voices we all hear in our heads that say "back off," "take the easy way," "be comfortable" and "don't know!" No sooner had Jesus made the commitment to walk his path than "demons" went into action! The gospel tells us that he "cast out demons." Jesus walked right through death itself to claim victory. It is by "walking in his footsteps," by facing our demons down, that we, too, will triumph over them. There is "new life" awaiting each victory.

How does one "enter" this transforming process? Put most simply, we must change the way we see. We must undergo radical "eye" surgery. We must radically change the way we interpret the things that happen to us. We must look at the same events with new eyes.

The entry point into spiritual growth could be anything that shakes our present world to the foundation; a heart attack, a divorce, a death, a serious illness, major surgery or sudden unemployment. The entry point might also be some unplanned encounter: a new book, an adult education course, a new acquaintance or maybe even a moving song or a great homily. It doesn't make a bit of difference whether the event was self-initiated, circumstantial or forced upon us. It is our attitude toward the experience that counts. If we embrace the experience, growth is possible. If we reject the experience, a little more of ourselves will wither away. These events can be understood as rocks that come crashing through the windows of our lives. The messages attached could be read as "Opportunity knocks!" The main thing is to keep making positive responses to each invitation.

There are numerous ways to respond to the "rocks" that come crashing into our lives. Some people respond to their "entry events" with the curiosity of children. This is the response Jesus advocates. "Amen, I say to you, whoever does not accept the kingdom of God like a child will not enter it" (Luke 18:17).

I have, over the years, observed people who respond this way. They are the widows who have a good, long cry and then courageously set out to create a new life. They are the amputees who push themselves to compete in the athletic world. They are the millions of AA members who celebrate their sobriety. One day a "rock" came crashing into their world, and somehow they got that spark of courage necessary to say "yes" to its invitation to change and to stand up to all the "demons" who tried to dissuade them.

Another way to respond to such entry events is to run. Those who respond this way are often people who are afraid of having to let go of some favorite old habits, afraid of losing control, afraid of having to revise their maps of reality, afraid of all the work that real change will require of them. Instead of directing their energy into finding the opportunity inside this new situation, those who run from them waste their energy on resisting this unwanted reality. They think to themselves: "If I just don't like this enough, maybe it will go away." These are the people who go through life fine-tuning their impressive list of reasons for not being happy: "If this had not happened...," "if it weren't for him or her...," "if it weren't for the times we live in...," or "I'm a victim of circumstances!"

One final example of the way numerous people respond to such entry events is to hesitate. Some people hesitate because of concern about how significant people in their lives might react should they seriously start to change.

Sometimes this hesitation and lack of curiosity is used as a defense. As much as we like to complain, often we don't really want things to be all that different. "What if I might have to become committed to some demanding discipline? What if I find out that what I really want out of life is radically different from what I have? What if I get 'caught up' in something, start having weird new experiences, or worse yet, even liking them?"

We both fear and crave becoming ourselves, being who we really are. Somewhere at each entry point we all have to make a decision. We can say "no," or we can say "yes." Those of us with second thoughts can say "no" and exit the process at any time. But if we say "yes," then things will never be quite the same. We are on our way to becoming a new person.

We have all had these "rocks" come crashing into our lives many times, whether we recognized them for what they were or not. These events may have been extremely painful, even tragic. They may have been mind-blowing, "eureka" experiences. How did we respond to them then, and how are we responding to them now? If we are ready for the adventure of spiritual and personal transformation, then we need to wrap our arms around the next opportunity and see where it takes us. We need to put some real passion into our search. We can become a new person as many times as we like, depending on how much courage we can muster and how much attention we can pay!

SETTING OUT

Given on March 7, 1993

*The Lord said to Abram: "Go forth from the land
of your kinsfolk to a land I will show you. Abram
went as the Lord directed him. Abram was
seventy-five years old when he left...*

Genesis 12:1, 4

It was about this time of year, several years ago, that Archbishop Kelly pulled me aside at a priests' meeting and dropped these words on me: "I want you to go to the Cathedral and do something with it! I'll give you a week or two to think about it."

Talk about a "rock" crashing through the window of one's life! I was a very happy country pastor of about 150 families. I had been there for only three years into what was supposed to be a ten-year assignment. I was comfortable and loved. The people were fabulous. It was a piece of cake!

I was completely stunned and completely caught off guard by the invitation. My mind was immediately inundated with negative chatter. "Why give up my cozy little parish in the country for an aging old landmark in downtown Louisville?" The Cathedral had only a handful of parishioners, a bag full of problems and very little money. What could realistically be done downtown besides hold Masses? The expectations are unrealistic! I'll just say "no!"

Along with that loud negative mind chatter was a small little voice in the back of my head that kept telling me to "try it" because I might just be able to do something. I knew then that if I didn't say "yes" I would always regret it, because I would always wonder what could have happened. I chose to listen to the small voice rather than the noisy mind chatter. After a few days, I wrote to the Archbishop and said "yes."

By the time I arrived here, I was fired up! I had two associate pastors and an engraved invitation from the Archbishop himself to be as creative as I wanted to be. My enthusiasm, however, was short-lived. I was so frustrated at the end of my first year that I wrote a letter offering to resign. The parish was so small that it was relying on tourists to pay the bills. All my ideas required new money. The only money the Cathedral had was in a guarded savings account, and the Chancery was so afraid that we would soon go through all our savings that they were reluctant to release to us what we had.

In a slow response to my letter, the Chancery finally released the money so that we could invest in some new programs, especially music and liturgy. Because cathedrals have a mission to the entire community, and not just to the parish and diocese, Cathedral Heritage Foundation, an interfaith foundation, was created a few years later in another response to my plea for help in the awesome task of revitalizing the Cathedral as spiritual center for the whole community. Gradually the parish started to grow. The Cathedral Heritage Foundation took off. Everything seemed to click! Each year of experimentation and exploration has produced results.

Yes, we have had some setbacks and frustrations, but as we are now about to enter the "big breakdown before the big breakthrough" that our major renovation project will bring, I can smell a dream coming true! I think we're going to make it, if we just hang in there a little while longer. We will have our revitalized congregation and our restored facilities. Then, when the renovation of the Cathedral church is finished, we will have to display a new kind of courage and imagination if we are to use it well and harvest its potential as a community-wide spiritual feeding center. For me, this whole adventure has been a personal spiritual transformation process and a communal process of growth that we have shared as a parish!

The beautiful story of Abram's call from our first reading today is perfect for today's subject. At age seventy-five, a "rock" came crashing into Abram's life. He and Sarah were comfortably retired, almost with one foot in the grave! Can't you just hear what was going on in Abram's head? "You want me to be a father for the first time, now? You want me to re-locate, now? I must be crazy for even giving this a second thought! What kind of crazy old man would say yes to something like this?" Being a man of faith, Abraham said "yes" to God. "Sarah, pack the suitcase! Buy some maternity clothes! Put on your walking shoes and follow me!"

The Gospel today presents us with another perfect story about spiritual transformation. I call it a "glimpse of glory." Jesus gives his disciples a preview, a taste, a glimpse of the glory to come. Like most people in the initial stages of transformation who get a first glimpse of what is to come, Peter wants to bottle it. "Hey, this is so good, let's just stay up here forever!" But the disciples had only a glimpse. To get from "here" to "there," they would have to descend into the valley of death and climb back out again. Jesus meant for this preview, this taste and this glimpse to sustain them during the rough times on the journey ahead.

We might call the second stage of spiritual and personal transformation the exploration stage. After saying "yes" to an entry event that offers us an invitation to growth and change, we set out (warily or enthusiastically) on an exploratory phase. Having sensed there is something worth finding, we leave one shore and set sail for another. No longer resisting or fighting the process, our mind courageously opens up to receive something new. An open mind is essential before anything can change. With this new openness, the adventure of transformation begins.

In the exploratory phase of spiritual growth, the seeker sooner or later gets a taste of the world to come and, liking the taste, becomes like a kid in a candy store. Like Peter in today's gospel, we want to make the taste permanent. The initial taste, the first success, is so empowering that he or she enters a period of "busy seeking." On one hand they experience exhilaration. They can't get enough of the new technique, teacher or program. They keep seeking to duplicate the initial, powerful experience. On the other hand, they feel loneliness. In this phase, they can become obnoxious evangelists, driven to tell the whole world of their newly discovered cure for all ills.

You know these people, those who go off to some monastery, shrine or program, have a charismatic experience, come home to unmercifully recruit new candidates for the experience (in between regular return visits themselves), and end up considering "going into it full time," all in a six month period! This is often a period of "obnoxious certainty" that has behind it a craving for others to validate the experience. This is Peter the Fisherman, bragging one minute and falling on his face the next.

If people don't burn out during this stage, or drive others crazy, they are ready to go deeper. The essential thing in this stage is not to give up, but to graduate. Graduating is about moving away from one point of view and finding a viewing point. They realize that no single system works for everybody, and so they concentrate on their path and allow others to find their own best way. From such a viewing point, we can appreciate not only our own point of view, but also many others' points of view at the same time.

Let me summarize the stages of spiritual and personal transformation I've discussed so far. In stage one, you are offered an entry point. You look at the entry point and either reject its invitation to grow and change or decide to embrace the opportunity that it presents. If you go with it, you enter stage two, a time of exploration. In this stage, you often have very powerful, moving experiences through which you get a glimpse of what is yet to come. These experiences can be almost narcotic, making you a little "nuts," but that's okay. It's part of the process. If you are patient with yourself and realize what it is, just a sample, you won't despair when it isn't permanent and you find out that there is still a lot of hard work to be done. You are ready to move into yet another phase: integration.

The transfiguration story from the gospels is very helpful to those in the second stage of spiritual and personal transformation. It reassures them that there is a place for these intense religious and personal growth experiences, even though they know they cannot stay on the summit forever; they have to come down again. So why bother in the first place? Because that which is above knows what is below, but what is below does not know what is above. One climbs, one sees, one descends; one sees no longer, but one knows that one has seen a "new place" to be.

In the transformation process, we at the Cathedral often get glimpses of what is yet to come, just like we did when the community space downstairs was finished or when the sample window bay was completed in the church, but in between these glimpses there is a lot of hard, dirty work to be done before we can realize our dream. These mountaintop experiences keep us going through the rough times. We can live by what little we have seen.

VALIDATION

Given on March 14, 1993

*"We no longer believe because of your word; for
we have heard for ourselves, and we know that
this is truly the savior of the world."*

John 4:42

Just look at this place! Dust! Peeling paint! Junk! Ugliness everywhere!

Last week, I was going through some old photographs and came
upon a shot of the church interior taken a year ago. It looked so
neat and clean and tastefully decorated. My mind went back to a
few months ago, to one of those stately and meticulously planned
celebrations we used to have around here. While I sat there looking
at the picture, my nose was feeling like an over-filled vacuum cleaner
bag from breathing all the dust we have around here, especially
during the weekdays. For a minute or two, I was having those feelings of wishing we have never even started.

I caught myself and chuckled, because I realized that I was having second thoughts, and I realized that those kinds of thoughts are
an integral part of any transformation process. They were right on
schedule! But I also know that during this part of the transformation process, the new will start showing itself, even in the dust. In
fact, I've been standing on a piece of the future for a couple of weeks
now. That is not a temporary platform. That *is* the front tip of the
framework for the new altar steps and platform. Like a crocus stick-
ing its head out of the snow, the new cathedral will evolve from all
this mess!

The perfect map for spiritual and personal transformers is, of
course, found in our first reading, the Book of Exodus. In this story,
the "people of God" find themselves enslaved in a foreign country.
This is all of us when life isn't working. Moses proposes to lead
them out to a "new land," into a new way of living. Moses is symbolic of the "rock marked opportunity" that comes crashing into

our lives. The people of God decided to follow Moses and accepted the invitation to move into a new way of living. But like all people in a transformation process, their enthusiasm turned to despair not too long into the trip. The old life, all of a sudden, began to look good in comparison to the discomfort of the "in-between world," symbolized by the desert.

Like all people in a transformation process, Moses' followers begin to regret ever having "set out" to begin with. From time to time along the way to the Promised Land, a few tidbits of hope seem to come out of nowhere — some water, some strange-tasting bread and even a few quail. They continued, in spite of the desert, only to realize one day that things suddenly began to get a little greener every day. Then finally, they make it! "Land ho! Can't you see it, ever so faint, on the horizon there?" They finally move into the new life they used to only dream about.

This is what should be expected in every spiritual and personal transformation. The steps are as certain as that spring follows winter. It's the way things work!

You get an opportunity to change, an invitation to growth. If you refuse to tolerate your own resistance, but rather accept this opportunity, be it painful or pleasant, you enter the process. You set out, optimistic that you can reach success by way of a slightly uphill path. You enter the process fueled with confidence.

Not too long into the process, "demons" jump around in your head or onto your path to frustrate your plans and trip you up. They try to make you lose sight of your goal or convince you that you have fallen into a hopeless situation. This is precisely where we all sink or swim in the transformation process. No guts, no glory! Just because things are not turning out as you had planned does not mean you should give up. This simply forces you to turn to your creative source and find an alternative way to get to your goal. Frustration is a necessary component of any transformation process. Do not make the mistake of giving up on your aspiration if you encounter what appears to be an impasse. Your response to this imagined impasse is what is truly important.

Many exit the process here. That's what all that whining is about in our first reading: they want to go back! "Why did you ever make us leave Egypt? Was it just to have us die here from thirst? At least we had plenty to eat in the old days!" If you expect and face such situations and hold your ground, you will begin to see solutions you never thought of. All of us going through the process of spiritual and personal transformation find ourselves in the shoes of the Israelites at some point or another. Unfortunately, we may have to go through several of these episodes during this phase. This is the stage marked with dissonance, sharp conflict, oscillation and testing.

Having triumphed over all the temptations to give up, go back and quit, another step opens up in the process. Breakthroughs and insights begin to pop like corn! They might come with a jolt of amazement or a simple, quiet knowing. Before you know it, you actually become the new person you set out to be. This is a period of new strength and sureness. This is the next step after all the messes, setbacks and frustration. This is what we will see evolving from the dust and destruction we see around us. This new strength and sureness will come, as surely as the spring will follow the winter. This is how it works, whether you are transforming a building or transforming yourself. The breakdown we are experiencing is the surest sign that a breakthrough is imminent. Pain is not a good reason to exit the process; it is the best reason to stay the course. Pain and chaos should come as no surprise in a transformation like this. In fact, it should be expected — we should plan on it.

Having survived one of these trips, you will end up back on level ground, enjoying your triumph, living in your new world or being your new self. And after you have survived a couple of these trips, you may find that you no long need to rely on "the program," "the guru" or the "leader." You will no longer need to trust them. You will know for yourself that the process works, and you will trust it enough to apply it to other areas of your life. You will begin to trust your own inner "guru." You will need less and less external validation. You will be like the people of Samaria in today's Gospel who said: "No longer does our faith depend on your story. We have heard for ourselves, and we know that this really is the Savior of the world."

Once you have been through the process a few times, you begin to understand how it works, and you know that each time you apply the process to some area of your life that isn't working or that you would like to change, you will inevitably go through an unsettling period of disillusionment, temporarily throwing you into a bottomless pit. You will have learned to expect it, and you know to ride this period out, realizing that victory is also inevitable. Here, the words of the Prophet Habakkuk come to mind: "For the vision still has its time, presses on to fulfillment, and will not disappoint; if it delays, wait for it, it will surely come, it will not be late." Habakkuk 2:3.

Having discovered how transformation works and having mastered the process, you are finally ready to start "throwing rocks through your own windows." You are ready to induce your own labor pains of growth and set out on one journey after another. Instead of being driven to accumulate more and more material benefits for yourself, your real love and passion in life will be for going deeper and deeper into yourself. Then you will have found the "pearl of great price," "the narrow door" and the kind of "wealth" that "moths cannot consume, rust cannot corrode or thieves cannot steal."

REPETITION

Given on March 21, 1993

*"Surely we are not also blind, are we?" Jesus said to them,
"If you were blind there would be no sin, but now you are
saying, 'We see,' so your sin remains."*

John 9: 40, 41

I cannot remember "the hour I first believed," but it seems to me
that I have given my heart and soul to religion for as long as I can
remember. I can still remember clearly struggling to memorize the
Our Father and Hail Mary when I was six years old. The idea of
becoming a priest came to me when I was seven years old. I joined
the seminary at fourteen years old. I was ordained at twenty-six
years old. I was thirty-one years old when I became pastor of my
first church and thirty-six years old when I became pastor of my
second church. I was thirty-nine years old when I became pastor
here at the Cathedral. It seems that I have given my heart and soul
to religion my whole life long.

While I would not trade my vocation with anybody, I am well
aware that being a priest these days is not easy. I have watched
most of my classmates leave the priesthood. I have been embarrassed by the constant stream of scandals in which my brother priests
have been involved, while I realize that "there, but for the grace of
God, go I." I have spent a mountain of energy trying to heal the
damage institutional religion has done to some people, while I
tremble to think that a slip-up of mine could cause another "to lose
their faith."

I have worked with one hand to make a place for the rejected and
marginalized in our church, while I work with the other hand to
bandage my own wounds and keep myself from coming unglued. I
continue to speak a message of hope to people who are a step or
two away from giving up, while fighting off the urge to quit myself.
I know from experience that it takes a special kind of courage to
stay in organized religion today. On a bad day, I am tempted to

believe that there are only two kinds of people left in the church — the sound asleep and the heroic saintly. "We walk by faith, not by sight" (2 Corinthians 5:7).

It pains me very much to see the church I have loved all my life undergoing so much trauma. But whether we like it or not, the old is passing away before our eyes. This has led many people to conclude, wrongly, that religion is dying.

In response, conservatives are trying to drag us back to the "flesh-pots of Egypt," which they imagine were the "good old days." "Conservatives" are learning that those who try to preserve their life will lose them even more of it. The ranting and raving about how they ought to be listened to is having less and less effect. They see "conformation," obedience to authority, as the answer. They even think they can get that obedience merely by demanding it.

"Liberals" are no help either, because they see the solution in more "reformation," the reorganization of religious forms. Iconoclasm, the careless destruction of religious symbols, is often the only agenda of some "liberal" religionists.

Both conservatives and liberals are overcome with discouragement these days because they both miss the point. They are both obsessed with external fixes. Religion is not dying, it is moving inside people, and that is hard to track with polls that measure external religious behavior patterns. For that very reason, I am extremely hopeful and optimistic.

Both conservatives and liberals miss the point, because what's wrong with us cannot be fixed from the outside. They have both forgotten that the authentic Christian message calls first of all for a change of heart, a radical internal change of the person. Obedience to authority and structural reform is not a means, but an outcome, of transformation! External actions will follow from a person's changed heart. Most religious authorities and political leaders haven't figured this out yet. The internalization of religion can neither be legislated nor demanded.

This series of talks has been about fixing things from the inside out, not the other way around. This "blindness," which results from focusing on changing things "outside," is what keeps us wallowing in despair and ineffectiveness. It is precisely from this "blindness" that Jesus invites us to be healed! Life does not unwind from the outside inward, but from the inside outward. When we make this transition in our thinking, we are ready to create miracles for ourselves and for our world. This series has been about how to change our lives and change our worlds from the inside out — about transformation. No church, no family, no country is strong when everyone in them is weak. Transformation, the internal change of individuals, is our only hope for better lives and a better world. We've tried everything else.

In these talks I have described an internal process. When we turn within to find the amazing spiritual powers of the mind, heart and body, we find out that God is not just "out there" somewhere, but with us – right here and right now. He is that presence "in him we live and move and have our being" (Acts 17:28). It is from within, where God lives, that we are called to transformation. I believe this "turn in thinking" is what Jesus called *metanoia*.

Let's review this process of transformation one more time. First there is the entry event, that event which I describe as the "rock that comes crashing through the windows of our lives," inviting us to change and grow. This entry event can be the death of a cherished person, a divorce, a job change, a new acquaintance, hitting bottom in an addiction, or a new book. It can be either painful or pleasant.

These events can be forced on us, be circumstantial, or be self-initiated. The only thing that matters here is our reaction to those events. If we embrace the experience of change, we enter a transformation process. If we resist, we join the masses of those who choose not to grow for the sake of safety and comfort, those who commit spiritual and personal suicide. But once committed to the process of transformation, we must undergo a painful breakdown. With patient endurance, this breakdown is followed by a breakthrough. Finally, we enter the "promised land." We become that new person; we find ourselves living the new life we used to dream about.

Those who have survived the transformation process a few times no longer need to rely on the reported religious experiences of others, for they know for themselves. They have had their own religious experiences. They are ready to apply what they have learned to many areas of their lives. Once they have become convinced of the effectiveness of engaging the process and mastering it, they are ready to become co-creators of their lives.

Maybe these spiritually maturing people got their first taste of transformation by embracing something that happened to them, but they now become ready to induce their own labor pains of growth. Instead of waiting for entry opportunities to happen to them, they are ready to "throw rocks through their own windows." When they reach this point, they are able to act boldly on their own behalf. They realize they can help themselves be happy. Believing in their own power and strength, they can make up their minds to begin a hero's journey of transformation. Believing in their own God-given power and strength, they know that the courage to face loss, transition or rejection will be there as they break down the boundaries around who they are, what they can do and what is possible. They look outside at the stars one night and realize that there is another world within them that is just as vast, an inner world that one can explore.

Some in our community who still believe that people are changed through *conformation* or *reformation* have always hated the fact that we will "take anybody" here at the Cathedral. They want to hear more about condemnation of behaviors, more about laws, more about obedience to authority from this pulpit. I choose to preach Jesus' "conversion through invitation" method. I believe that the world can only be changed from the inside out.

In these talks, I have sought to share what I have discovered with you — the power of spiritual and personal transformation. I prefer being a guide to being a judge. Transformation cannot be imposed on those who are not ready for it, but it can be made available to those who are hungry for it. I will not be discouraged that this series of talks has not changed the world. I am excited by the fact that some of these seeds have already sprouted in some of you. Positive reports are already coming in. I realize that I have no control over the outcome. That's between you and God! My job is merely to plant seeds!

A PASSION FOR PASTORING

A Call Within a Call

A PASSION FOR PASTORING

A Call Within a Call

… It becomes like a fire burning in my heart …

Jeremiah 20:9

The idea for this chapter actually came out of my own experience of being a new pastor. I was made pastor five years after ordination, something very rare in 1975. I was given two counties and told to start two Roman Catholic mission parishes in an area where Catholic parishes had never been.

I was prepared to be an urban associate pastor, but I was not prepared to be a pastor for the first time, to live alone or to start a parish, especially in the "home missions." I hardly knew what the word "evangelization" meant, much less how Catholics did it. Neither was I prepared for the pastorates that followed at a well-established rural parish and a center city cathedral.

With little help, support or direction available to me, I decided to teach myself. I decided that I was going to find the help I needed and to teach myself, if need be, so as to become the best pastor I could be. I decided to develop a "passion for pastoring" and to see where that took me. As I learned later, from the experts, self-directed learning is the crux of leadership development. Pope John Paul II put it this way — all formation, including priestly formation, is ultimately self-formation.

Any priest, I believe, who has a "passion for pastoring," will look for every opportunity possible to learn what he needs to learn to be an effective pastor.

In that light, let me now say a few words about the "passion for pastoring" that I have been talking about, because being a pastor is, in a sense, a vocation within a vocation.

Diocesan priests are called from the laity to live among the laity, so as to empower the laity in their baptismal priesthood. Priests are not priests one by one, but serve the church as a team, in a presbyterate, under the leadership of the bishop. All priests carry out the ministry of the bishop. From this body of priests, the church calls certain priests to be pastors. Unlike an associate pastor who helps the pastor carry out his ministry, the pastor has a special obligation to preserve the community's common good, as well as the good of its individual members. The pastor is responsible for the unity of the flock, not just the welfare of individual sheep.

As such, a pastor needs to move from a personal point of view to a viewing point so that he can appreciate not only his own point of view, but also the various views of the community. The Congregation for the Clergy has made it clear that a priest can never put himself at the service of an ideology or human faction. Pastors are the primary ministers of communion in the community, something that is sorely needed in our badly divided church. Unlike a seminarian, or even an associate pastor, a pastor does not have the luxury of a point of view, but needs to hold in unity a variety of legitimate points of view.

Priests have as their primary duty the preaching of the gospel, along with presiding at the celebration of the sacraments and leading the community, but as pastor a priest has the additional task of overseeing the preaching and sacramental ministries of the parish, as well as the leadership ministries of the parish. As pastor of our Cathedral, I used a simple formula that worked well. I encouraged creativity within set boundaries. It is the role of the pastor to set boundaries around creativity, lest the crazies take over the asylum.

Being a pastor today requires an imaginative and entrepreneurial attitude, outlook and approach. As I said earlier, when I became a pastor five years into priesthood, I was not prepared, and there were no programs available at that time to prepare me. In those days, priests learned to be pastors by observation, over 15-20 years, as associate pastors under a series of seasoned pastors. My situation back then would be the norm today. Young priests are becoming pastors of multiple parishes in a very short time, without a lengthy internship and without programs in place to train and support them.

In the absence of that normal series of seasoned mentor-pastors or how-to-be-a-pastor programs, I decided to hunger and thirst for being a good pastor. I decided not to wait to be rescued by the diocese or even find people in the Chancery to blame. I made up my mind to find a way on my own. Leaping over obstacles and using my best imagination, I committed myself to becoming the best pastor I could be.

I even turned to Protestants for help and financial support. I got a Doctor of Ministry degree in "parish revitalization," and I got the Presbyterian church to pay for it on two grounds: minority religion and poverty income! Being a pastor today often takes that kind of determination and imagination.

Even "new pastor programs" don't have a chance in hell unless they attract young priests who have a passion for pastoring. All ongoing formation of this kind is the responsibility of the individual priest. He must be a self-starter, self-motivator and self-rescuer, if need be. He must summon up all the determination, imagination and creativity he can muster. He must crave with all his heart to be a "good shepherd," an effective pastor. "Where there is a will, there is a way."

Being a pastor requires special skills. Unfortunately, those skills are not infused at ordination. They are earned through deliberate intention, concentration, education, reflection and practice.

A "passion for pastoring" is ultimately a spiritual gift that can be asked for, embraced and cultivated through prayer. God never calls people to spiritual leadership without also giving them the ability to do the job. Like Solomon who prayed for all he needed to be a good king, those who are called by God to be pastors will get what they pray for. Like Gideon who prayed to know how he could possibly do what God asked, we are told that God will be with us if we seek, knock and ask for what we need to be a good pastor. Through prayer, it will be given to us, running over into our laps. Having the people pray for us, as pastors, is also a good suggestion. A pastor's spiritual leadership depends on it.

There are two possible words in Greek for good: *agathos* and *kalos*. In the gospel text about the "good shepherd," *agathos*, meaning "morally good," is not used. *Kalos*, meaning "good at," is the word used here. Jesus, the Good Shepherd, is not only morally good, he is especially good at shepherding. As a person who stands in persona Christi, you too are called not only to be good, but also to be good at pastoring.

On the other hand, a pastor who acts *in persona Christi* is certainly called to be holy. Father Howard Bleichner makes this point: "How much difference one holy person who seems transparent to God's presence makes! Is there any more adequate sacramental vessel, a monstrance of God's presence, than a human personality suffused with the love of God? Is there anything more riveting, more justifying of the church's existence than a single person in whom holiness of life has found a home?"[65]

However, such personal goodness and holiness is not enough. A pastor is also called to be "good at shepherding." He neesd to be "good at" preaching the Word, "good at" presiding at the sacraments and "good at" leading the community. Vatican II told bishops that, "in making a judgment on the suitability of a priest for the administration of any parish, the bishop should take into consideration not only his knowledge of doctrine but also his piety, apostolic zeal, and other gifts and qualities necessary for the proper exercise of the care of souls."[66]

The skills of a pastor include skills in communication and administration. Pastors need practical wisdom to translate general norms into particular situations. They need presence and availability to their people. "I am the Good Shepherd. I know mine, and mine know me" (John 10:14). Pastors need to have a sense of the whole. They need spiritual transparency or an evident spirituality that enables them to be unambiguous witnesses of the holy mysteries they proclaim and celebrate.

A pastor also directs, guides, manages, and governs the parish as a system, a community. The American Bishops spelled out these skills in greater detail in their *Basic Plan for the Ongoing Formation of Priests.* "A pressing need for a new pastor is to acquire the "know-how" of being and functioning as a pastor. Often, this is tied to very specific issues, for example, the business function or pastoring. Pastors need to learn basics of financial management, fundamental personnel management, conflict resolution, the organization of meetings, community organization and communication, and the management of volunteers. Pastors need to familiarize themselves with canonical requirements, diocesan regulations, and any legal provisions that have a bearing on parish life, such as employment law. Finally, new pastors need to discover ways of knowing and understanding the community in which they serve: demographics, culture, economics, and political realities."[67]

Today's pastor, then, needs not only to be personally holy, but he needs also to have a set of precise skills, if he is to be effective. He must be "good" and "good at" it.

Being named a pastor is not just about getting a new job or acquiring a fancy title or personal honor; it is the beginning of a great spiritual adventure wherein one not only learns how to pastor, but how to be sufficiently centered spiritually. Appointment to a pastorate propels a priest into new growth and development. The time of entering the first pastorate is a moment ripe for ongoing formation in all its dimensions. Appointment to a pastorate intensifies the challenge of integrating who the priest is and what he does as a priest. The words of Paul to the presbyters of Ephesus is a simple outline of the task of pastoring, "Keep watch over yourselves **and** over the whole flock of which the Holy Spirit has appointed you overseers..." (Acts 20:28).

Father Bleichner makes another great point in his book. He says that, because of the shortened time between ordination and first pastorate, training in the skills to be a pastor must begin in the seminary. Seminaries must endeavor to train men not just as priests, but also as pastors, almost from the start.[68]

This will mean a new look at the vital and unbroken connection between the initial formation of the seminary and the ongoing formation after seminary. What is offered in the seminary does not yet prepare young men to be pastors any more than medical schools prepare doctors to be trained surgeons. In the absence of such established and coherent programs, the individual pastor-to-be (at least in the near future) needs to take personal responsibility for his own pastoral education and commit himself to it with all the passion he can muster.

The title of "pastor" will not of itself make a priest into a leader. Designated leaders are people who have the titles and robes of a leader, but not necessarily the appeal and skill of a real leader. When that appeal and skill are absent, designated leaders who are not real leaders eventually have to pathetically appeal to their status. Sheep recognize the voice of the one who is "good at shepherding." Real leaders have something to offer besides their position. They do not need to rely solely on their titles and robes. The best-case scenario is when designated leaders are also real leaders, people recognized as leaders with obvious ability to lead their flocks into ever-expanding discipleship.

What is the essence of good pastoring? Is it merely good management? Certainly not! People clearly and urgently want priests to pull themselves out of themselves and out of their in-house, intra-ecclesial squabbles and preoccupations. They want substance and hope. They want Jesus Christ and salvation in a world marked by sin, division, violence and death. They plead with priests, "Show us Jesus. Give us bread. Touch us and heal us. Forgive and renew us." They want priests to be spiritual leaders with a heart for the people of God. Our capacity to respond will depend in large measure on our preparation to serve in this way and the ongoing formation that will **keep** preparing us to serve in this way.

The pastor most likely to be successful in spiritual leadership is one who leads not merely by pointing the way, but by having trodden the path himself. The People of God want to follow a "martyr," a "witness," someone who has "walked his talk."

Pastors who are spiritual leaders are not just religious policemen. When a pastor demands obedience of another, he is a tyrant. But when, by tact and sympathy, compassion and prayer, inspiration and wisdom, a pastor is able to influence and enlighten another to alter his course and pursue a spiritual one, he is a spiritual leader.

Pastors who are spiritual leaders work on themselves, discovering and correcting their weaknesses, as well as discovering and cultivating their strengths. In short, spiritual leaders are always working to increase their ability to influence others.

Pastors who are spiritual leaders cannot produce spiritual change themselves; only the Holy Spirit can do that. Transformation cannot be taught, but it can be modeled and encouraged. Pastors as spiritual leaders can, and must, strive to be worthy and effective conduits for the Holy Spirit. They are catalysts in the chemistry of the spiritual life.

Pastors who are spiritual leaders do not blame their followers when they do not do what they should do. Instead, they work to improve their ability to influence. They hone their skills and keep trying. Many pastors, poor at pastoring, have left their parishes blaming their people for their own failures.

Pastors who are spiritual leaders can influence not just church people, but all people. Pastors are leaders in the church, but also in the civic community at large.

Pastors who are spiritual leaders work out of compassion and love, never anger and despair. A sure sign of failure in the spiritual leadership of a pastor is when he looks back and sees that no one is following him.

Pastors who are spiritual leaders believe so much in the intrinsic value of what they do that they keep working regardless of the outcome. As Mother Teresa put it, "We are called to fidelity, not results."

Pastors who are spiritual leaders have integrity and transparency, knowing that they cannot achieve a noble goal by using ignoble means. Pastors as spiritual leaders have private lives, but not secret lives. Secret lives drain energy away from the task at hand. As their ordination rite as a deacon puts it, they are to be heralds of the gospel who "believe what they read, teach what they believe and practice what they teach." They cannot serve two masters at once.

Pastors who are spiritual leaders do not demonize their adversaries. It is wise for them to entertain alternative points of view because there is usually a kernel of truth even in what their enemies affirm. What they affirm is often a pastor's blind spot. This kind of openness is where growth happens.

Pastors who are spiritual leaders lead for the sake of others, not for their own satisfaction or benefit. As the Catechism of the Catholic Church (no. 1535)[69] says, if priesthood makes priests holy, it is in serving others that it does so.[5] Pastors who are spiritual leaders know that it is in giving that they receive. Pastors who are spiritual leaders know that they are helped through their helping. A great spiritual leader always knows that he has received more than he has given.

Pastors who are spiritual leaders do not insulate themselves from the pain of the world. They know that "compassion" means "to suffer with." Pastor-priests are called from the laity, to live among the laity, so as to empower the laity. As they experience the pain of those they serve, they are more able to become better vehicles of transformation.

Pastors who are spiritual leaders rely on deep faith and God's promise of victory over sin and darkness. They know that the kingdom will come, no matter what, and it is growing like a mustard seed or yeast in dough, regardless of our ability or inability.

In short, pastors who are spiritual leaders lift, inspire and call: lift people's vision to God, inspire people to become better disciples and call people to become all God has called them to be.

A CARE-FILLED
ENTRY INTO A
PARISH

———— ∾ ————

A CARE-FILLED ENTRY INTO A PARISH

Remove the sandals from your feet, for the place where you stand is holy ground.

Exodus 3:5

Not every priest knows how to enter a parish well. "Fools rush in, where angels fear to tread."[70] Some newly ordained priests, as well as some new pastors, in their "beginner's zeal" and in their eagerness to use all they have learned, enter parishes like bulls in a china shop. I can still remember being embarrassed when I was referred to as "brash" in an article in our diocesan paper when I was about to be ordained. "Brash" means "lacking restraint and discernment to the point of arrogance." It is a perennial, all-too-common, trait among newly ordained priests and inexperienced pastors.

In their impetuous mission to fix what is wrong, some priests use a hatchet to remove flies from people's foreheads. Like the well-intentioned "weeders" in the parable of the weeds among the wheat, they think they can tell weeds from wheat and are more than willing to "get to work," only to find out too late that they were misguided. Sometimes their cocky boldness is merely silly, but sometimes they do irreparable harm to people and lose years of goodwill that might have made them effective sooner, rather than later. Many priests, new to parishes, are shocked, surprised and disappointed when they discover that their collar alone is not enough to carry the day when parishioners disagree and have other ideas.

The first rule, when it comes to entering a parish, is this: It is *their* parish, not *yours*. Since it is *holy* ground, a priest must take off his shoes. He must stop, look and listen. Before He starts judging, stereotyping and trying to "fix" people, he needs to let them tell him who they are, where they are coming from, how they feel about themselves and what is going on in their lives. This needs to be done it without judgment, by just listenening and taking it in. If this is done, trust will begin to be built, and *then*, and only then, will they themselves begin to listen.

People really listen only when they can identify in some way with the person who is talking. If not, there is no real communication. This identification is absolutely essential to trust and credibility. If people cannot identify with a priest, they do not give credibility or trust, no matter how much he thinks he has to give.

Who are these people? A parish priest stands in the presence of people of every conceivable level of faith. He celebrates with people who are already giving their lives in service to their spouses, children, neighbors and fellow parishioners. He looks at people who have been through years of old, experienced love and people filled with the wonder and excitement of fresh, young love. He faces rich people and poor people, the well-off and the cast-off. He is being watched by the esteemed and the rejected. There are people before him who have been nurtured by the church and people who have been hurt by the church. But, most of all, he has people who are all touched by the uncertainty of life, sickness, suffering, dying, separation, loss, rejection, loneliness and alienation. And if he is truly *wise*, and not just *smart*, he will know that he cannot see into hearts and will not evaluate people by externals, coming to judgmental conclusions about which he knows very, very little.

After 37 years of priesthood, one begins to notice what works and what doesn't. In no certain order, I offer a short list of attitudes a priest should carry into ministry from day one.

WANT WHAT YOU GET

Seldom do priests get exactly what they want in their assignments. Therefore, it is important for them to learn how to make themselves want what they get. Even though a particular parish community may be assigned to a priest, hopefully he can decide to consciously choose that parish community as his own. In every parish, but especially in rural and struggling parishes, the priest will need to let his parishioners know on a regular basis that he is happy, lucky and honored to be their priest.

One of the practices that has worked, everywhere I have been assigned, is greeting parishioners at the door of the church every Sunday and seeing them off at the door after Mass, in fair weather and foul. This has been the single most effective pastoral practice of all.

Another practice is making it a personal policy to regularly affirm parishioners in my homilies. A priest can't do that until he means it. If he doesn't mean it, a change of heart might be in order. People know in their guts whether or not they are liked. If they know a priest loves them, they will hear his voice and follow him. If not, his words may fall on deaf ears.

PAY ATTENTION TO INDIVIDUALS

One of the first things to slide with busy, over-extended pastors and associate pastors is the personal touch, that one-on-one attention that people need and respond to so positively. In a very small parish, it is relatively easy to know what is going on among the parishioners. In a huge parish, it is almost impossible.

One of the most effective ideas I have ever come up with to help me maintain a personal touch in a large parish is to recruit a volunteer to assist me in paying attention to individual parishioners. This volunteer's job was to skim the newspaper, committee minutes, school newsletters and any other sources of information on our parishioners. It was their job to draft cards and letters of thanks, sympathy or congratulations for me to sign. As my eyes and ears, they helped me pay attention to those I am sent to serve. It was so effective, it bordered on "magic."

Priests are notorious for not returning calls, following up on requests and expressing thanks for gifts. It may be necessary to recruit some help to get this done, but there is no excuse for not doing it.

SPEAK THE TRUTH WITH LOVE

What parishes need desperately today are priests who are bridge builders, peacemakers, reconcilers and mediators of unity. Priests need to be able to deal constructively with diversity, pluralism, complexity, ambiguity, division and polarization. Those who would exercise leadership in the church are called to be ministers of healing communion. The church needs, especially today, priests whose words heal rather than wound, who express themselves with sensitivity for the dignity and worth of every person. Civility, as one priest said, is not just a civil virtue. The church today needs civility badly and nowhere more desperately than among its priests.

Even though a policy of encouragement and affirmation should be a priority among parish priests, there are times when a challenge is called for from the pastor, especially when the common good is threatened by a few. Even though such challenges are not easy or popular, they are the truly loving thing to do. The secret is to speak without anger, false judgment or recrimination. A "good shepherd" "speaks the truth with love."

The style of leadership on the part of the priest is one of service. He is to be a servant to the People of God, holding them accountable for what they have been and can be. He serves them by calling forth leadership and coordinating ministries. "Holding them accountable" must be done with love and patience, never with anger or meanness.

LET THE PARISHIONERS BE THE TEACHERS

Priests sometimes give the notion that they are the only ones with something to teach or give. As the main "coordinator of charisms" in the parish, a priest must acknowledge and affirm the many and varied gifts within the community. Priests need to be open to being students as well as to being teachers. Priests are not the only people in the church with gifts to give.

People take ownership of the mission of the parish when their talents, gifts and expertise are called on and used. To do this, the priest must understand that his role is to empower others, to serve instead of being served. The priesthood is not an institution that exists alongside the laity or "above" it. The priesthood of bishops and priests, as well as the ministry of deacons, is "for" the laity, and precisely for that reason it possesses a ministerial character, that is to say, one "of service."

RESPECT THEIR HISTORY

Every priest is a hero to somebody. No matter what a disaster a priest, or others, feel the former pastor or his associates might have been, he needs to speak respectfully of them and their work and let people know up front that he has come to build on the good work of others, not to be their "savior." He should let them come to that conclusion, if they must, *after* he leaves.

CONCLUSION

In my experience, if a priest enters a parish exuding love, honor and respect for the people he serves, they will in turn love, honor and respect him. "The measure with which you measure will be measured out to you" (Luke 6:38). If a priest loves, honors and respects them and their history, they will afford him that same love, honor and respect. In fact, they will give it back "pressed down, shaken together and poured into your lap" (Luke 6:38).

Catholics still want to love and respect their priests, but these days it is the individual priest's gift to lose.

A CARE-FILLED EXIT
FROM A PARISH

—— ⅊ ——

A CARE-FILLED EXIT FROM A PARISH

Great is the art of beginning, but greater is the art of ending.

Henry Wadsworth Longfellow

One common failure of spiritual leaders is not recognizing when to quit. It is better to leave them longing than leave them loathing. It is better to go out in a parade than on a rail.

In many dioceses there are term limits for both pastors and associate pastors. These policies were adopted because, in the past, especially, a pastor could spend his whole life in one parish. Often that was good for the priest, but bad for the people. However, the coming of term limits did not eliminate creative ways of trying to hang on. Some priests try to set up situations to extend their stay, while others meddle after they leave. Both are symptoms of the inability to let go.

It takes leaders with great integrity and spiritual insight to recognize when they have made their most worthwhile contribution and to graciously turn over the reins to another. Sometimes the energy coming from the parish sends a clear message. The facts speak for themselves. It is pathetic to watch priests who did great jobs years ago stubbornly refuse to let go long after they quit being effective, and who end up undoing much of their own work. There is a spiritual art in knowing when one's time is up.

Another common failure of spiritual leaders is that they spend little time or effort preparing their congregations for their departure.

People do not fear change — they fear loss. Nothing can be as upsetting to priests and parishioners alike as an unexpected change in pastoral leadership. Resistance to change comes from a fear of the unknown or an expectation of loss. Not enough attention has been paid to these fearful feelings of loss, especially in Catholic congregations who have so little say about who comes, who goes or how long they stay. An individual's degree of resistance is determined by whether they perceive the change as good or bad, and how severe they expect the impact of the change to be on them.

Managing change inevitably means managing fear. This is an important last ministry that priests can perform for their people. A priest who is "good at pastoring" addresses the fear and resistance of his congregation when it comes to the leaving of a pastor, not just his own fear and resistance. With care and faith, he can "talk them through it."

Below I have included a series of homilies that I gave when I made the transition out of the Cathedral of the Assumption in Louisville, Kentucky, after fourteen years of service. The parish had grown from 110 individuals to more than 2,300 individuals. We had just finished a $22,000,000 restoration. I was told that I could stay as long as I wanted. I knew in my heart of hearts that I had given it all I could, so I "induced labor." I actually asked to resign. It was traumatic for them and me, so I decided to talk them and myself through it by comparing our transition to the transitions of the early church after the death and resurrection of Jesus. It is a homily series on the importance of embracing necessary change. It was followed a few weeks later by a final "goodbye" homily.

"THE CHALLENGE OF CHANGE"

PART I: Looking Back, Looking Forward"

God has brought to fulfillment ... what he had announced.

Acts of the Apostles 3:18

Ever since I announced that I would be leaving the Cathedral this June, I have been bouncing off the walls, emotionally. Part of me wants to hang onto the old and familiar. Part of me is anxious to embrace the unknown and yet to be. One minute my mind is going over some part of the last fourteen years, and the next minute my mind is dreaming up ideas for my new job. One day I'm thinking about all the things I'll miss; the next day I'm thinking about the new opportunities I am about to encounter. Part of me wants to hang on. Part of me wants to let go. I'm afraid to let go. I'm afraid to grab onto the future.

This has been my home, and you have been my family, for the last fourteen years. To leave you and this beautiful place and start all over again at age 53 is a little traumatic for me. With one foot in one world and one foot in another, I find myself looking back and looking forward. Even though I know it's for the long-term good, I feel as if I am being pulled up by the roots. Even though I have had several weeks to get used to the idea, I know the worst is yet to come. I know that when it's all over and the goodbyes are complete, I'll probably have to close my door and have a good cry!

As we go through this together, I thought I'd take advantage of the fact that I will be preaching at all the weekend Masses for the next month to reflect on the challenge of change. This four-week homily series will try to glean some wisdom about change from our post-Easter Scripture readings. These readings tell us about the monumental and painful changes that the early church went through as it grew and spread after the Resurrection. I believe they have much to teach us as we go through our changes.

One of the things that stands out in today's readings is the fact that the disciples were in between two worlds: one *with* Jesus and one *without* him. For forty days, Jesus appears one minute and disappears the next. They are looking *back* and looking *forward*. They are talking about the past and talking about the future. Peter tells his audience, "The God of Abraham, of Isaac, and of Jacob, the God of our fathers [and mothers] has glorified his servant Jesus… God has brought to fulfillment … what he announced long ago…" (cf. Acts 3:11-21). Jesus reminds his disciples, "These are my words that I spoke to you when I was still with you, that everything written about me in the Law of Moses and in the prophets and psalms must be fulfilled" (Luke 24:44). It is obvious that they struggled to put in perspective all the changes that surrounded them.

Jesus and his disciples had become a close-knit group in the three and one-half years they were together. They hated to see it end — hated it! Peter put it quite well in the "transfiguration story." "Let's put up three tents and stay up here forever." In other words, "Let's freeze this moment together and make it permanent." Jesus reassures them with his gift of peace. He empowers them with the Holy Spirit, tells them they will do what he did and even greater things still, and promises to be with them always. Even after 2,000 years, the church is still here, the church is still carrying on the work of Jesus under the power of the Holy Spirit and the church is still changing, still struggling with letting go of the past and embracing the future. And so it will be, until the end of time. The church is not a museum with everything frozen in time and preserved in dusty cases. It is alive. And it is alive because it always builds anew on its past. As St. Paul puts it, "One person plants and another waters, but it is the Lord that brings things to fruition."

Everyone here today has probably gone through, is going through or will go through similar, painful changes. Some of you parents will be walking your children down the aisle and "giving them away" in a wedding ceremony. You know in your heart that your relationship with them will never be the same. An old way of relating to them will die, as you watch a new relationship develop. More often than not, even though it will be necessary, it will also be painful. Some of you have, or will have to, roll your spouses down the aisle and "give them away" in a funeral. You know in your heart that things will never be the same. An old way of living will die, as a new way of living develops. More often than not, even when it is necessary, it will be painful. Some of you have been, or will be, hauled into court to face a divorce. You know in your guts that life will not be the same. An old way of living will die, as a new way develops. Like it or not, it will be painful. Some of you will be hauled into the front office and handed a pink slip. An old way of living will die even before a new one appears. Like it or not, it will be painful, and it will have to be faced. Some of you will be hauled into a nursing home, sell your home and surrender an old way of living. Like it or not, it will have to be accepted, and it will hurt. The examples could go on and on, be it retirement, the break-up of a relationship or a terminal diagnosis. The question, then, is not whether things ought to change, but how one deals with inevitable changes.

Change, welcomed or un-welcomed, is always a challenge. Those who have won the lottery say that even that can bring disruption and confusion. Welcomed or un-welcomed, when confronted with change, we have two choices. We can fight it and deny it, or we can embrace it and explore it. Denial in the face of necessary change, however human and natural, exacts a terrible price, wastes time and ultimately doesn't work. An awesome amount of energy goes into avoiding and denying unwanted change. Conserve that energy and use it to embrace that change, and watch it reveal something else that is beautiful and life-giving. It really is a matter of attitude. Jesus taught us this when confronted with his cross. He was tempted to try to avoid it, to find a way around it, but by choosing to reach out and embrace it, he triumphed over it.

When I look back over my life, some of the greatest and most marvelous outcomes have come about by embracing changes that appeared to be disasters. When I was ordained, I was sent against my will to the missions of our diocese. I hated the idea. I begged and cried and pouted. In a moment of grace, I decided not to fight it, but to embrace it and explore it and see where it would take me. Thank God for that grace-filled decision! It made the difference between ten miserable years and ten of the most growth-filled years I had experienced so far in my life. In 1983, I was pastor of a small, comfortable country parish. Archbishop Kelly asked me to make a change, even though I had only been there three and one-half years. He wanted me to leave that comfortable nest and take over this run-down, dying parish. My first impulse was to say "no." In a grace-filled moment I overcame my fear and said "yes." Thank God for that grace-filled decision. I would have missed out on all the marvelous things that have happened here in the last fourteen years! And now, we are faced with another change, a change that we could have put off for a few more months or maybe another year, but one we would have had to face sooner or later: a new pastor for this parish. As painful as it will be, I believe with all my heart and from all my experience that by embracing this necessary change we will open up new possibilities for both of us: as Vocation Director, I can try to do something about our priest shortage, and your new pastor can take what we have built together and take it to yet another level of life.

As we look back to the past — be it the Cathedral parish, your children's childhood, a marriage that is over through divorce or death, a job or relationship that has ended — let us face our fears, embrace the facts, cry a little if we have to and then finally open our hearts to something new from God. Yes, the best could be yet to come, if we can only bring ourselves to believe it and proceed as if it's true until it comes true.

"THE CHALLENGE OF CHANGE"

PART II: "Cloning Shepherds"

The good shepherd lays down his life for the sheep. A hired man who is not a shepherd has no concern for the sheep.

John 10:11-13

Someone asked me recently, "What is the thing you are most proud of as you leave the Cathedral? Is it the beautiful renovation of the church? Is it the establishment of the Cathedral Heritage Foundation? Is it the collection of homilies you published? Is it the huge growth in the number of parishioners?" As proud as I am of all these things, I told her, none of them are the one thing I am most proud of. Those things are obvious and visible to the eye. What I am most proud of is invisible, immeasurable and has taken place in the hearts of individuals. What I am most proud of is the fact that a significant number of you have told me that you feel, for the first time in your life, that your religion has finally become life-giving, real, exciting and personal, and that you credit my preaching for being the catalyst for that happening. That's what I am most proud of. I've always thought that that's what being a "priest," in the best sense of the word, really means: being a catalyst, a conduit, a channel, a medium, a connector — between God and people.

For the last 14 years, I have been your "pastor." The word "pastor" is Latin for a "shepherd." Traditionally, the role of the shepherd is to oversee the feeding of sheep: to lead them to where the best grass and the cleanest water is to be found. The shepherd does not make the grass and create water. He just knows where to find it. It is the role of the sheep to eat and drink when they get there. The shepherd cannot do that for them. In other words, you can lead sheep to pasture, but you can't make them graze! As your "pastor," I have worked very hard to offer you the best spiritual nourishment I could from this pulpit, to teach you what I know about the spiritual life and to show you how to graze in the green pastures of your own spiritual life. I never served you "leftovers." And because I knew that I would not be around forever, because I know there is a shortage of spiritual teachers, I have deliberately tried to teach you how to feed yourselves, how to find your own spiritual food, how to do without a shepherd if you have to and finally, besides shepherding yourselves, how to be a shepherd to other hungry sheep. We hear a lot these days about cloning sheep. What we need even more, and what I have tried to do, is to clone shepherds: people who can guide others to the joys of being wide awake on a spiritual journey.

Those who have been here for a long time know that I have pushed and pleaded and begged you to take responsibility for your own spiritual and personal growth. I have always thought that the greatest compliment you could pay me is to get to the day when you no longer need me, or at least could do without me. There are several signs that we have come a long, long way in that area.

Over the last year or two, there has been a movement from the grassroots of this parish to join with others for personal, spiritual growth.

Several support groups have formed and are thriving: the young adults support group, the middle age support group, a youth group and an expanded senior group. Last week, we had four more parishioners graduate from the Archdiocesan Ministry Formation Program. Once a month a large group of Saturday night lay ministers goes out to eat together and to enjoy and support each other. The best part of these groups is that, unlike all the older programs, which came from the staff out, these came from you.

The successful beginning of our Cathedral School of Catholic Spiritual Growth and Education, a structure where serious spiritual seekers can deliberately nourish themselves through interaction and education, excites me very much. We now have a small cadre of married couples who mentor our young couples who are about to get married, to share their wisdom and offer their support. Another group of volunteers is being formed to take on some of the small maintenance projects around here.

For years and years, I have prodded and pushed you to take responsibility for your spiritual life and for this place. I am convinced that you have heard me. It makes me proud that some of my sheep have now become shepherds. There are other shepherds here who know what I am talking about. Parents, you spend the best years of your life trying to make your children independent of you and able to stand proudly on their own two feet. Teachers, you spend years trying to make your students go even farther than you did and make great contributions to the world. Spouses, married love is about coaxing out all the goodness you can in each other. Seeing your partner advance and bloom should be the joy of your heart.

I guess all of us shepherds have this one goal in common: making those we lead able to do without us, summed up in that trite old maxim, "Give a person a fish and he eats for a day. Teach him to fish and he will never go hungry." We know when we have been successful: our sheep don't need us any more. The thing I am most proud of is this: A few years ago, I deliberately set out to lead you to where the green grass and fresh water are, spiritually. Many of you can now find spiritual food on your own. In fact, a few of you are beginning to teach others how to find it. How do I know this? I have a huge stack of letters from you, saying so. Let me end this homily by quoting from just two of those.

"I don't know if I can manage without you but I believe the Cathedral Parish can. You have energized them into being a strong, independent, vital group. They'll do well because you gave them a foundation upon which to build. It's sort of time, then, isn't it, that you move on, sharing God's word with others and stirring up vocations?"

"You have also been there for me, whether you are aware of it or not, through your sermons and the congregation that you have drawn together. We who sit quietly in the pews Sunday after Sunday are growing inside. You must see us growing as you look out on the congregation. We'll miss you, Father. But what you have begun will continue to grow. The dynamic, inclusive parish that you have formed will flourish. With such concepts as you have given us of the unconditional love of God, how could it not?"

I am proud of you. That's what I'm most proud of. Keep shepherding yourselves and keep shepherding each other. Invite people in. Teach what you've been taught. Make the circle bigger and bigger!

"THE CHALLENGE OF CHANGE"

PART III: "Connected and Interdependent"

I am the vine, you are the branches. ...
without me you can do nothing.

John 15:5

Last Sunday night, I was honored to speak at one of our "young adult support group" meetings. They had submitted 12-13 questions that wanted me to answer: questions that ranged anywhere between "how to develop a personal spiritual life" to "how to remain faithful to the church when you have problems with it." Before I started to answer their questions, I noticed something very interesting about these questions. Most of them focused on the needs, the rights and the freedoms of individuals. I pointed out to them that the generation ahead of them would probably have asked a completely different kind of question: questions that focused on the needs, the rights and the freedoms of the community. One is not better than the other. Both can be taken to extremes. The "me generation" was, I believe, just an over-reaction to the previous generation that tended to obliterate individuality.

I have been a part of both generations. In my early seminary training, individuality was something the seminary system tried to break us of. It was the good of the group that was valued as essential. Individuality was rooted out for the sake of group needs. In my later seminary training, individuality was something that was so exaggerated that any kind of rules, uniformity or structure almost became anathema.

One generation seems to try to correct the exaggerations of the last generation when it comes to the balance of personal good and the good of the group. I actually saw it happening before my eyes last Sunday night: a room full of healthy young adults, children of the "me generation," working to form themselves into a small community for mutual support. I think we may have turned a corner! Maybe this time, we'll find the middle of the road, a good balance between the good of individuals and the good of the group.

If the Bible has one thing to say on this subject, it is this: we are individuals, but we are also intimately connected to God and to each other. It is to our detriment if we should forget or ignore this fundamental fact. All sin is, in one way or another, a denial of this fact. Even the "original sin" was not really about eating forbidden fruit, it was about an attempt to ignore the fact that God, human beings and the animal-material are connected and interdependent. Every sin after that was just a variation on the same theme: whether it is Cain denying that he was his brothers keeper, Israel denying its covenant with God, the religious wars and social injustices of our modern world or the irresponsible personal behaviors all around us that tear marriages, families and neighborhoods apart.

The Bible is really the record of God telling human beings about their place in a delicate relationship of interdependence and human beings' constant refusal to accept that fact and live in its truth. The motif of "the vine and its branches" in today's gospel is one more attempt to describe the special, life-giving relationship we have with God through Jesus. It reminds us that "connected" we have life; "cut off" we wither and die. St. Paul's image of the body of Christ states the same thing about the family we call the church. We are not individually the Body of Christ. All of us — no matter how insignificant we may feel about ourselves or how badly we may be treated by others — are interconnected parts of one body. St. John puts it bluntly: Whoever says he loves God, without loving fellow human beings, is a liar!

Interdependence is not a halfway point between dependence and independence. Interdependence means an active relationship based on mutual respect and shared responsibility for the common good. The opposite is egocentrism. Egocentrism, as its name suggests, means being self-focused. Attention and interest are constantly focused on the self. All acts, endeavors and relationships have as their primary purpose enhancing or protecting the self in some way. Since our own needs are seen and felt to be more important than the needs of others, interaction with others tends to be self-serving. Egocentrism is a self-perpetuating cycle: the more we focus on ourselves the less we know about others.

The less we know, the less we care and the more we focus on ourselves. Viewing the world through an egocentric frame of reference means that everything we do or hope to do is important only if we feel we gain from it. How it affects others is eclipsed by how it affects us. Violence, crime, child abuse, poverty, homelessness, rape, murder, profits over people, massive casual abortions, quickie marriages and easy divorces are simply the fruits of an egocentric culture. Our present self-focused world view is just another severe case of the "original sin," the failure to accept our interdependent relationship with God and each other.

We see this in the attitude that many Catholics have toward their parishes. In the last several years, Catholics quit thinking about what they can do for their parishes and have started to focus on what their parishes can do for them. An interdependent parish is one where people are nourished and give nourishment, in a life-giving cycle, one based on the wisdom of Jesus, "It is in giving that you receive."

As I leave this parish as your pastor, I have one challenge for you: Take responsibility, not only for your own spiritual growth, but also for the health of this parish. If you want this "golden goose" to keep laying "golden eggs," feed it, care for it and nurture it, and it will continue to feed you and those around you. But if you come here only to take, you will kill this "golden goose" and it will no longer provide you and others you with "golden eggs." It seems that every Catholic I meet is looking for a life-giving parish, but often they want someone else to provide it for them. A life-giving parish is an intricate system of give and take, a delicate balance of interdependence, a family where mutual respect is given and shared responsibility for the common good is accepted.

Besides taking care of each other, as a Cathedral parish, you have a mission to serve others beyond yourselves. As the "mother church" of the diocese, you have a special responsibility for reaching out to all the parishes of the diocese. Because of our location, you have a special responsibility to be a spiritual center in the heart of downtown, a responsibility that goes beyond Roman

Catholic boundaries. Raise your eyes and look around you. Take your mission seriously. Keep the three-fold mission that we have defined and revitalized over the last few years alive and growing. Attend to each other's needs. Co-operate with the Archdiocese. Work with the Cathedral Heritage Foundation. This is your vocation as a parish. Egocentrism, being self-focused and coming only to get, will be the death of this parish. Interdependence, an attitude of give and take, mutual respect and responsibility, will insure that this parish will be life-giving for many for years to come. In the words of Jesus, "What you have been given, give as a gift" (Matthew 10:8).

Just because I am leaving here, as your pastor, does not mean that our connection will be severed. Part of me will always be here, and I will carry part of you wherever I go. Now, open your minds and hearts to the gifts that Father Fichteman will bring. Work with him to build on the foundation we have laid together. You're going to like him, because he has lots to offer, gifts we need to go to the next level. He's the right person at the right time!

"THE CHALLENGE OF CHANGE"

PART IV: "The Island of Misfit Toys: Revisited"

It was not you who chose me, but I who chose you...
love one another.

John 15:16-17

Somebody asked me a few weeks back if all the harassment of demonstrators, anonymous "white paper" attacks and vicious pamphlets had anything to do with my decision that it was time to leave the Cathedral. I chuckled because I had never even thought of that. The answer is a resounding "NO!" They did throw me into small episodes of self-doubt and make me re-think my position, but I always ended up more convinced than ever that our policy of not only of welcoming the marginal and minorities, but also actively reaching out to them, was right out of the gospel. Besides, those kinds of attacks are signs that we are doing the right thing. In fact, the brighter the light, the fiercer the attack. The response to our invitation has been so good that I was shocked that the attacks were not worse than they were. The people they attacked are one of the main reasons I stayed four years longer than I was supposed to stay. I am very proud that we are a parish where the marginal and minorities feel at home.

Yes, I consider it a badge of honor to be attacked for reaching out and welcoming the marginal and minorities. This conviction is not something that came to me from some kind of liberal social agenda. This conviction came from my reading of the gospel and my own spiritual journey. I grew up shamed. My father told me from day one that I was stupid, incompetent and that I probably would never amount to a "hill of beans." Many of my religion teachers, who had probably been shamed themselves somewhere along the line, combed the Bible for condemning messages and built a distorted little religion around those messages.

The minor seminary system was built on the idea that if one dug up all of a person's flaws, sins and shortcomings and dwelled on them night and day, one could get a person to change. I was even told in the seminary that I was a hopeless case and that I probably should not be a priest. In reality, all this had the opposite effect. I ended up feeling worse and worse about myself and feeling further and further away from God. I lived in fear: afraid of other people and afraid of God.

My best was never good enough for my dad, for some of my seminary formators or, as I once thought, for my God. The message from both was: be perfect and we'll love you. Since I could not be perfect, no matter how hard I tried, the only thing left for me to do to have peace of mind was to avoid my dad and avoid my God with all their condemning messages. It seems the more condemnation I got, the more alienated I got. I was never motivated to change by condemnation, and I have never met anyone who has been, even though some self-righteous Christians believe their mission is to ferret out sinners for condemnation.

At some point I began to read the gospels, really read them. The Jesus that I found there was radically different than the Jesus that had been filtered for me. Jesus, in the gospel, ferreted out sinners not for condemnation, but for love. Jesus worked his transformation on people by, first of all, accepting them as they were. He did not say, "Get your act together and then come and see me." He loved the lost sheep just as much, if not more, than the 99 who stayed together. He loved his prodigal son just as much, if not more, than his model son who never did anything wrong. His closest friends were people who were left out, cut off and on the edges. This caused the self-righteous to gossip, "This man welcomes sinners and even eats with them." The ministry of Jesus in the gospel is summarized for me in the line from the Second Eucharistic Prayer for Reconciliation, "When we were lost and could not find our way to you, you loved us more than ever."

I was personally transformed by this message of unconditional love on God's part, something that the old, condemning, sin-obsessed messages were never able to do. It gave me a base, a place to start building myself into a better person. Yes, I know that I can make mistakes, but what I have discovered is that I am not JUST one big mistake. There is a world of difference in the two. People who don't understand that accused Jesus of condoning sin, just as we have been for welcoming "rejects" into this parish.

This discovery, like finding the pearl of great price, has had such a profound affect on my personal life. In the words of Jesus, "What I have been given as a gift, I want to give as a gift." I have preached this message from this pulpit for 14 years; you have supported and joined me in promoting this message, and the response has been phenomenal. A whole lot of broken people have been healed in this welcoming and accepting climate, people who had all but given up on the church, people whose lives are still transforming under its power. I have boxes of letter to prove it.

As I leave here in a few weeks, my hope and prayer is that this ministry, the ministry of reaching out and welcoming the marginal, minorities and rejects, will remain the heart of the Cathedral's ministry. Years ago, someone called us the "Island of Misfit Toys." That comes from a "Rudolph, the Red Nosed Reindeer" TV Special. The "Island of Misfit Toys" was where dolls with one eye, toy trucks with one wheel missing and teddy bears with one ear were sent. In the story, even defective and broken toys get to be part of Christmas. Even divorced, gay, fallen-away Catholics, as well as any other so-called "rejects," I believe, are loved by God and deserve a home in the church. I am proud that I have been part of that welcoming committee these last 14 years. Don't stop delivering that message, even after I am gone, because as the lady said, "You never know who and when you are reaching someone" who really needs to hear it and feel it. It changes lives in a way that condemnation never does!

FINAL HOMILY

"Goodbye"

Tenth Sunday of Ordinary Time

"Because I believed, I spoke."

2 Corinthians 4:13

"There is an appointed time for everything, and a time for every affair under the heavens. A time to be born and a time to die; a time to weep, and a time to laugh. ... a time to be silent and a time to speak" (Ecclesiastes 3:1-8). To that familiar quote, I might add "a time to say "hello," and a time to say "goodbye." Now is the time for me to say "goodbye."

Today we mark the end of one adventure and the beginning of another. You will continue your spiritual journeys under the direction of a wonderful new pastor. I will go on sabbatical, finish another book, teach preaching at Saint Meinrad and, in January, become a traveling evangelist and vocation director. All such endings and new beginnings are fraught with fear, insecurity, doubt and a measure of sadness. What we are feeling is not unique. "The leap into new spaces is never made in comfort." We will need faith, courage, patience and hope. Let's trust that the God who calls us to set out anew will provide what we need to make this transition.

In our second reading today, Paul has just finished reviewing the ups and downs of his ministry for his Corinthian congregation. As we take up the reading, Paul notes that it is his passionate faith that drove him to share what he had experienced with others. His preaching comes out of deep conviction. He is compelled to preach. "Because I believed, I spoke."

As I reflected on my own ministry here at the Cathedral, I found myself sharing some of Paul's thoughts about preaching. From all the generous feedback I have received from you, it seems that we have "clicked" because what has been most life-giving for me, preaching the Word, has been life-giving for you, hearing the Word. What I have enjoyed doing the most is what you have appreciated the most. I have worked very hard on my preaching during the years I have been here, as have several associate pastors, including Father Linebach. Like Paul, I have learned one important thing about preaching since I've been here: preaching has to come from in here (heart), not just from up here (head). That comes about through prayer, introspection and self-examination. Therefore, good preaching transforms not just the hearer, but also the one who preaches.

I have in front of me five of my most prized possessions. If my house ever caught on fire and I had the chance to save something, I would without a doubt run through the flames to rescue these things. They are, by far, the most valuable things I own.

(1) The first pile is my spiritual journals. They represent the work I've done on myself over the last 14 years. From the moment I arrived here, my faith was challenged. I was told by several people that I should not get my hopes up because "nothing can be done about the Cathedral: its days are numbered." I remember deciding not to accept that advice, that lack of faith. In spite of the odds, I deliberately chose to believe that something was indeed possible if we could only bring ourselves to believe. So I committed myself to operate out of faith, rather than throw up my hands in despair, no matter how dismal the signs were in 1983! To maintain my faith, I kept spiritual journals in which I talked myself into belief, encouraging myself to faith. I have learned a very important lesson in keeping those journals: when one, day in and day out, "trusts God, believes in himself and dares to dream," miracles do happen. I plan to use this technique in my new job, another so-called "hopeless situation:" the so-called "priest shortage." I recommend this technique to those of you who are facing your own so-called "hopeless situations."

(2) Out of that struggle, believing in God, believing in myself and believing in you, I "spoke out." This second pile represents

14 years of "speaking out" about God's unconditional love for all of us. I believe that I still have about 99% of all the Sunday homilies I have written during my years with you. As you can see, I have many of them on tape as well. Besides all these homilies, I produced one book and six spiritual growth tapes. I have preached 15 parish missions and mailed out, across the country, 70 printed copies of homilies each week. Those of you who sent me tips and gifts for this service, I want you to know that I put your gifts in a "preaching endowment," which now totals about $30,000. Use it to invite the best preachers you can find to the Cathedral.

(3) The third pile is your letters to me, giving me feedback and encouragement. I have never been in a place where Catholics have shown their appreciation so openly. Because you took the time to express your thanks and offer your encouragement, I was motivated to do my very best and try as hard as I could to offer you quality spiritual nourishment. You have prodded me to grow; you gave me the strength to keep going when I was up to my ears in alligators, and you have made my priesthood a joy, something that brings me deep happiness and something I want to recommend to as many young men as I can in the next few years. There is no way I can tell you how important it is to take the time to encourage priests these days. There is no way I can thank you enough for doing that for me. You have given me encouragement, "full measure, pressed down and running over into my lap" (Luke 6:38).

(4) This last folder is what I call my "humility file." I am very aware of my failures, sins and shortcomings while I was here. These are the letters in which people have expressed their anger, disappointment and frustration with me when I lost my patience, was too strict with the staff, failed to notice your hurts or simply "screwed up." It reminds me of an old Roman tradition when famous conquering generals returned to Rome in triumph. As they rode through the streets in their chariots with a crown on their heads to the applause of the populace, two things were done to keep it all from going to his heads. The people not only shouted their applause, but they also shouted, "Look behind you and remember you will die." Second, at the very end of the procession

some of their own soldiers would shout insults to keep them from too much pride. And so to those of you who wrote these nasty notes, I also have to say "thanks." You've played a valuable role, too. If I have hurt anyone, please forgive me!

And so it is time to say "good bye." For several months now, I have been asking myself, "How do you say 'goodbye' to those you love?" The answer I have come up with is to simply say "thank you." I thank the Archbishop for taking the risk of offering the Cathedral pastorate and trusting this pulpit to me when I was only 37 years old. He has been incredibly supportive. I thank the dedicated priests who have been partners with me in this ministry: Fathers Vest, Griner, Badgett, Medley, Stoltz and Linebach. Father Marty, stand up! Thank you for all you have done for this parish and for me. Thank you, too, for enduring the crazy side of my personality. Thank you for staying on. You deserve applause.

I thank our deacons, especially Pat Wright, his wife Sandy and family. You are solid gold! I thank the dedicated members of the staff who have also been partners with me, both those who have moved on as well as those who are still here. The list is too long, but there are a few long-time staff members who deserve to be singled out: Julie Zoeller, David Lang, Pat Sexton, Larry Love, Elaine Winebrenner, Jerre Basset and Shirley Jones. I thank the Parish Council presidents (Alice Hession, Ted McGill, Bob Tichey and Tim Bode) and numerous council members. I thank the hundreds of parish volunteers.

A humongous "thank you" goes to Christy Brown, who made our Heritage Foundation a national model and gave us this beautiful church. (By the way, it has just won a prestigious national AIA award for liturgy and preservation.) I thank the Cathedral Heritage Foundation Board, staff, committee members and volunteers of all religions. A very special thanks goes to Trish Pugh Jones and Susan Griffin, executive directors.

A big kiss goes to that small band of "little old ladies," especially Sodality members, who first welcomed me, mothered me and spoiled me rotten over the years.

Finally, I thank Father Bill Fichteman, who has the courage to take over this awesome responsibility and move it to a new level. Remember, he is leaving the people he loves to come here. Welcome him, encourage him, help him and love him, as you did me!

At the end of Mass today, I have a surprise farewell gift (a cross made from old Cathedral flooring with a home blessing engraved in it) for you, so stay around. I will finish here by quoting one of the cards I got a few weeks ago. It seems to say it best. It showed Snoopy with the words, "You'll never be far away." On the inside, Snoopy has his paw over his heart with the words, "You'll never be far away, because you'll always be right here." Thank you from the bottom of my heart! Thank you! Thank you! Thank you!

CONCLUSION

———— ✺ ————

CONCLUSION

People aren't looking for information about God. They want to experience God himself. Information leaves them bored, uninterested. Experience, especially the ultimate experience any human being can ever have, leaves them breathless. And that's exactly what we have to offer.

Mission to Oz[71]

The most pressing problem facing Catholicism today may just be the quality of its priestly leadership in the face of seemingly deteriorating religious devotion and faith, community cooperation, generosity and concern for the poor.

Organized religion has lost its power to impose unquestioned rules on the behavior of its members. No amount of ranting and raving from leadership about how it ought to be listened to, and no amount of new editions of the rulebooks, will fix this. Such fits are simply counter-productive, and the church is up to its ears in new rulebooks already.

Instead of blaming themselves for their lack of skills of persuasion, and a lack of dynamism in the church's own pastoral structures for evangelization in a changing cultural climate, clergy persist in their propensity to blame the laity for their lack of faith and the culture for its "secularism" and "moral relativism."

Instead of blaming others, the better approach might just be for the clergy to start owning the fact that the real problem may be their own style, mistakes and inability to influence others. Instead of looking *around* for a solution, maybe the clergy should start looking *within*. Designated spiritual leaders need to become real spiritual leaders.

Because of the nature of their preparation for ministry, priests tend to define themselves in relationship to the institution, thus keeping it dominant in their lives. They come to leadership with theological education, extensive relationships with bishops and fellow priests, institutional loyalties, and with personal and institutional administrative aims largely foreign to the experience of those they serve. The agendas of bishops, priests, seminarians, and even permanent deacons and career church workers for that matter, are often not the agendas of the laity.

The people with and among whom they serve have a different agenda. They are typically preoccupied by matters of day-to-day existence: birth, death, sickness, arguing and reconciling, falling in and out of love, hospitality and farewell, sustaining their own and their family's lives. They are also distracted and consumed by American popular culture.[72]

Because of this disconnect, many of the laity tend to think priests somewhat elitist because of their training, subtly aloof because their primary relationships are often elsewhere, and relatively inscrutable or tedious because of their institutional loyalties. Many priests tend to dismiss the aspirations and opinions of the laity when they are so deeply committed to the institution's, or their own, aims. "Effective and productive leadership will emerge from being in constant touch with the center, life where it is lived by the faithful, with their shared grass-roots experiences and leadership styles."[73]

In spite of these collisions of focus, the ordained are sent to call the people to conversion of life in Jesus Christ and to inspire, lead, and walk with them in their efforts to sort through the gifts and demands of their relationship with God, while the faithful are hungry for what priests have to offer and look to priests to show them the way to greater meaning, brighter hope and deeper peace. This is the gap that effective spiritual leaders need to close, because the People of God already know that what God wants is for us to be made holy (cf. Hebrews 10:10).

In a certain and real sense, any parish priest who wants to become an effective spiritual leader needs to overcome the downside of his isolationist formation. He needs to realize in a very practical way that he is called from the laity, to live among the laity to serve the needs of the laity. To be an effective spiritual leader, he needs to move from his own institutionally focused agenda to the agenda of the people he serves, to "the down-deep things," as Gerard Manley Hopkins called them.

"The priest is placed not only *in the church* but also *in the forefront of the church*."[74] "To whom much is entrusted, much is expected" (Luke 12:48). "A priest must have *logos*, enabling him to sustain reasons for his way of life. He must also have *ethos*, the transparent moral character, to persuade. He must finally have *pathos*, the ability to touch feeling, to move people emotionally from his own experience.

If a man cannot relate easily to most people — men and women — he certainly will not be successful in priesthood. If he has significant communication problems with others, the same is true. Similarly, the lack of healthy psychosexual maturity sustaining the gift of celibacy points to an unhappy life ahead. If he cannot see authority as cooperative discernment, a life of collision with superiors and those he serves lies ahead. Should his defective faith experience lead him toward extremes of secularism or fundamentalism, his priestly leadership will be seriously defective."[75]

In a society in which being a consumer is a primary self-definition, the priest has to know how to hustle, to be innovative, to be a self-starter, to spark imagination, to sell, to move from a vision to the details of execution. [76]

"Seminary life disguises the amount of initiative and energy and conflict resolution needed... [and] the amount of spiritual and practical effort required to sustain parishes and ministries... The challenge facing seminaries, then, is to introduce more reality into these institutions... ."[77]

80

BIBLIOGRAPHY

BIBLIOGRAPHY

Abbott, Walter M., SJ, ed. The Documents of Vatican II. New York: Guild Press, 1966.

Aschenbrenner, George A. SJ. Quickening the Fire in Our Midst: The Challenge of Diocesan Priestly Spirituality. Chicago: Loyola, 2002.

St. Augustine, In Jo.ev. 5, 15: PL 35, 1422.

Bennis, Warren. Why Leaders Can't Lead. San Francisco: Jossey Bass, 1989.

Biber, Rev. Jay. "Preparing Seminarians for an Emerging Paradigm of Priestly Leadership." Seminary Journal (Spring 2003): 48.

Blackaby, Henry and Richard. Spiritual Leadership: Moving People on to God's Agenda. Nashville, TN: Broadman and Holman Publishers, 2001.

Bleichner, Howard P. SS. View from the Altar. New York: Crossroads Publishing, 2004.

St. Bonaventure. The Character of a Christian Leader (originally entitled The Six Wings of the Seraph). Translated by Philip O'Mara. Ann Arbor, MI: Servant Books, 1978.

Catechism of the Catholic Church. 2nd edition. Washington, DC: USCCB, 2000.

Christus Dominus. In The Documents of Vatican II, edited by Walter M. Abbott, SJ; translation editor: Msgr. Joseph Gallagher. New York: Guild Press, 1966.

Code of Canon Law. Washington DC: Canon Law Society of America, 1999.

Collins, Jim. Good to Great. New York NY: Harper Collins, 2001.

Congregation of the Clergy. Directory for the Life and Ministry of Priests. Vatican City: Libreria Editrice Vaticana, 1994.

The Priest and the Third Christian Millennium, Teacher of the Word, Minister of the Sacraments, and Leader of the Community. Washington, DC: USCCB, 1999.

Coulter, Reverend Gary. "The Presbyterium of the Diocese." Homiletics and Pastoral Review. San Francisco, CA: Ignatius Press, 1905.

Cozzens, Donald B. "The Spirituality of a Diocesan Priest." In Being a Priest Today, edited by Donald J. Goergen. Collegeville, MN: Liturgical Press, 1992.

Dei Verbum. In The Documents of Vatican II, edited by Walter M. Abbott, SJ; translation editor: Msgr. Joseph Gallagher. New York: Guild Press, 1966.

Dent, J. M. The Scottish Himalayan Expedition. London, 1951.

Fowler, James W. Stages of Faith: The Psychology of Human Development and the Quest for Meaning. San Francisco: Harper and Row, 1982.

Gaudium et Spes. In The Documents of Vatican II, edited by Walter M. Abbott, SJ; translation editor: Msgr. Joseph Gallagher. New York: Guild Press, 1966.

St. Gregory the Great. "Pastoral Care." In Ancient Christian Writers: The Works of the Fathers in Translation, No. 11, translated and annotated by Henry Davis, S.J. New York, NY: Newman Press, 1978.

St. Gregory of Nazianzus. Select Orations, Sermons, Letters; Dogmatic Treatises. In Nicene and Post-Nicene Fathers. Grand Rapids, MI: Eerdmans, 1955.

Heher, Rev. Michael. The Lost Art of Walking on Water: Re-imagining the Priesthood. Mahwah: NJ: Paulist Press, 2004.

St. Ignatius of Antioch. First Epistle to the Ephesians. In Kleist, James A., The Epistles of St. Clement of Rome and St. Ignatius of Antioch. Mahwah, NJ: Paulist Press, 1946.

Jackson, W. Carroll. God's Potters: Pastoral Leadership and the Shaping of Congregations. Grand Rapids, MI: Eerdmans, 2006.

John Paul II. Apostolic Exhortation "Pastores Dabo Vobis." Libreria Editrice Vaticana, 1992.

Jones, L. Gregory and Kevin R. Armstrong. Resurrecting Excellence: Shaping Faithful Christian Ministry. Grand Rapids, MI: Eerdmans, 2006.

Kasper, Walter Cardinal. Leadership in the Church: How Traditional Roles Can Serve the Christian Community Today. Translated by Brian McNeil. New York, NY: Crossroad Press, 2003.

Leavett, Rev. Robert SS. "The Formation of Priests for a New Century." Seminary Journal, no. 3 (2002).

Lumen Gentium. In The Documents of Vatican II, edited by Walter M. Abbott, J. Translation editor: Msgr. Joseph Gallagher. New York: Guild Press, 1966.

Moorman, William, OSST. Response to J. Edward Owens, OSST, "Inside/ Outside the Camp: Places of Encounter." Human Development 27, no. 2 (2006): 36-67.

O'Donnell, Rev. Desmond, OMI. "The Anatomy of a Vocation." Seminary Journal, NCEA (2003): 75-79.

Papesh, Michael. Clerical Culture. Collegeville, MN: Liturgical Press, 2004.

Paul VI. Encyclical Letter "Ecclesiam Suam." Vatican City: Libreria Editrice Vaticana, 1964.

Peck, M. Scott, MD. The Different Drum: Community and Peacemaking. New York: Simon and Schuster, 1987.

Philibert, Paul J., OP. Stewards of God's Mysteries: Priestly Spirituality in a Changing Church. Collegeville MN: Liturgical Press, 2004.

Pontificale Romanum. De Ordinatione Episcopi, Presbyterorum et Deaconorum, Chapter II, nn 105, 130. Edition Typica Altera, 1890.

Presbyterorum Ordinis. In The Documents of Vatican II, edited by Walter M. Abbott, SJ. Translation editor: Msgr. Joseph Gallagher. New York: Guild Press, 1966.

The Record. Archdiocese of Louisville, June 16, 2006.

Rosetti, Stephen J. The Joy of Priesthood. Notre Dame: Ave Maria Press, 2005.

Sacrosanctum Concilium. In The Documents of Vatican II, edited by Walter M. Abbott, SJ; Translation editor: Msgr. Joseph Gallagher. New York: Guild Press, 1966.

Sanders, J. Oswald. Spiritual Leadership: Principles of Excellence for Every Believer. Chicago: Moody Press, 1967, 1980, 1994.

Schuth, OSF. Priestly Ministry in Multiple Parishes. Collegeville, MN: Liturgical Press, 2006.

Shaw, (George) Bernard. Man and Superman: Dedicatory Epistle to Arthur Bingham Walkley. New York: Brentano's, c1903.

Tabb, Mark. Mission to Oz. Chicago, IL: Moody Publishing, 2004.

Unitatis Redintegratio. In The Documents of Vatican II, edited by Walter M. Abbott, SJ; Translation editor: Msgr. Joseph Gallagher. New York: Guild Press, 1966.

United States Conference of Catholic Bishops. The Basic Plan for the Ongoing Formation of Priests. Washington, DC: USCCB.

Warren, Rick. The Purpose Driven Church. Grand Rapids, MI: Zondervan, 1995.

Waznak, Robert P. SS. "Homily." In The New Dictionary of Sacramental Worship, edited by Peter E. Fink SJ. Collegeville, MN: Liturgical Press, 1990.

Wills, Garry. Certain Trumpets: The Call of Leaders. New York NY: Simon & Schuster, 1994.

END NOTES

END NOTES

[1] Donald B. Cozzens, "The Spirituality of a Diocesan Priest," Being a Priest Today, Donald J. Goergen, ed. (Collegeville, MN: Liturgical Press, 1992), 51.

[2] The Record, Archdiocese of Louisville, June 16, 2006.

[3] St. Gregory the Great, "Pastoral Care," in Ancient Christian Writers: The Works of the Fathers in Translation, No. 11, trans. Henry Davis SJ (New York, NY: Newman Press, 1978), 21.

[4] Rev. Desmond O'Donnell, OMI, "The Anatomy of a Vocation," Seminary Journal (Winter 2003), 75-79.

[5] Warren Bennis, Why Leaders Can't Lead (San Francisco: Jossey Bass, 1989) 36, quoted in Henry & Richard Blackaby, Spiritual Leadership: Moving People on to God's Agenda (Nashville, TN: Broadman & Holman, 2001), n 2.

[6] Moorman, William OSST, Response to J. Edward Owens OSST, "Inside/Outside the Camp: Places of Encounter," Human Development 27, no. 2 (2006), 36-67.

[7] Gregory the Great, "Pastoral Care, "23-24.

[8] Ibid. 27-28.

[9] Ibid. 41, 54.

[10] St. Gregory of Nazianzus. "Orations," in Select Orations, Sermons, Letters; Dogmatic Treatises: Nicene and Post-Nicene Fathers. Grand Rapids, MI: Eerdmans, 1955), 39.

[11] Howard P. Bleichner SS, View from the Altar (New York: Crossroad, 2004), 63.

[12] Gregory the Great, "Pastoral Care," 45, 48.

[13] In this chapter, I have relied on many of the good insights found in J. Oswald Sanders, Spiritual Leadership: Principles of xcellence for Every Believer, (Chicago: Moody, 1967,1980, 1994) and its spin-off: Henry and Richard Blackaby, Spiritual Leadership: Moving People on to God's Agenda, (Nashville, TN: Broadman and Holman Publishers, 2001).

[14] St. Bonaventure, The Character of a Christian Leader, originally entitled The Six Wings of the Seraph, trans. Philip O'Mara (Ann Arbor, MI: Servant Books, 1978), 4-7.

[15] Quoted in J. M. Dent, The Scottish Himalayan Expedition (London: 1951).

[16] (George) Bernard Shaw, Man and Superman: Dedicatory Epistle to Arthur Bingham Walkley (New York: Brentano's, c1903).

[17] Unitatis Redintegratio, Walter M. Abbott SJ, ed., The Documents of Vatican II. (New York: Guild Press, 1966).

[18] John Paul II, Apostolic Exhortation "Pastores Dabo Vobis" (Libreria Editrice Vaticana, 1992), no. 69.

[19] Presbyterorum Ordinis in Abbot, Documents of Vatican II, nos. 7-8.

[20] See Rev. Gary Coulter, "The Presbyterium of the Diocese," in Homiletics and Pastoral Review (San Francisco, CA: Ignatius Press, 1905).

[21] United States Conference of Catholic Bishops, The Basic Plan for the Ongoing Formation of Priests (Washington, DC: USCCB, 2001), 97.

[22] Pontificale Romanum, De Ordinatione Episcopi, Presbyter-orum et Deaconorum, chapter II, nn 105, 130 (edition typical altera, 1890) 54: 666-67; Presbyterorum Ordinis, no. 8.

[23] Congregation of the Clergy, Directory for the Life and Ministry of Priests (Vatican City, 1994), no. 27.

[24] Presbyterorum Ordinis in Abbot, Documents of Vatican II, no. 6.

[25] United States Conference of Catholic Bishops, Ongoing Formation of Priests, 93.

[26] John Paul II, Pastores Dabo Vobis, no. 16.

[27] United States Conference of Catholic Bishops, Ongoing Formation of Priests, 97-98.

[28] Saint Ignatius of Antioch, Ephesians 4:1.

[29] John Paul II, Pastores Dabo Vobis, 28.

[30] Ibid.

[31] Ibid.

[32] Ibid

[33] Ibid.

[34] Lumen Gentium in Abbott, The Documents of Vatican II.

[35] Catechism of the Catholic Church, 2nd edition (Washington, DC: USCCB, 2000), no. 1534.

[36] Presbyterorum Ordinis in Abbott, The Documents of Vatican II, no. 9.

[37] Congregation for the Clergy, The Priest and the Third Christian Millennium, Teacher of the Word, Minister of the Sacraments, and Leader of the Community (Washington, DC: USCCB, 1999), 36.

[38] Paul VI, Encyclical Letter Ecclesiam Suam, 1964.

[39] Presbyterorum Ordinis in Abbott, The Documents of Vatican II, no. 4.

[40] St. Gregory the Great, Pastoral Care.

[41] Ibid.

[42] Presbyterorum Ordinis in Abbott, The Documents of Vatican II, no. 4

[43] Presbyterorum Ordinis in Abbott, The Documents of Vatican II, no. 4.

[44] Dei Verbum in Abbott, The Documents of Vatican II, no. 21.

[45] Gaudium et Spes in Abbott, The Documents of Vatican II, no. 62.

[46] John Paul II, Pastores Dabo Vobis, no. 26.

[47] George Herbert[48] This section draws on the article "Homily," by Robert P. Waznak SS in The New Dictionary of Sacramental Worship. ed. Peter E. Fink SJ (Collegeville, MN: Liturgical Press, 1990), 552-558.

[49] Sacrosanctum Concilium in Abbott, The Documents of Vatican II, no. 11.

[50] St. Augustine, In Jo.ev. 5, 15: PL 35,1422.

[51] Sacrosanctum Concilium in Abbott, The Documents of Vatican II, no. 11.

[52] Ibid.

[53] Ibid., no 14.

[54] Presbyterorum Ordinis in Abbott, The Documents of Vatican II, no. 5.

[55] John Paul II, Pastores Dabo Vobis, no. 17.

[56] Congregation for the Clergy, The Priest and the Third Millennium, 35-36.

[57] Ibid.

[58] Presbyterorum Ordinis in Abbott, The Documents of Vatican II, no. 9.

[59] Code of Canon Law (Washington DC: Canon Law Society of America, 1999), no. 545.

[60] Presbyterorum Ordinis in Abbott, The Documents of Vatican II, no. 8.

[61] John Paul II, Pastores Dabo Vobis.

[62] Presbyterorum Ordinis in Abbott, The Documents of Vatican II, no. 9.

[63] M. Scott . Peck, The Different Drum: Community and Peacemaking (New York: Simon and Schuster, 1987), 186-200.

[64] James W. Fowler, Stages of Faith: The Psychology of Human Development and the Quest for Meaning (San Francisco: Harper and Row, 1982).

[65] Bleichner, View from the Altar, 159.

[66] Christus Dominus in Abbott, The Documents of Vatican II, no. 31.

[67] United States Catholic Conference of Bishops, The Basic Plan for the Ongoing Formation of Priests (Washington, DC: USCCB, 2001), 72.

[68] Bleichner, View from the Altar, 58.

[69] Catechism, no. 1535.

[70] Alexander Pope.

[71] Mark Tabb, Mission to Oz (Chicago, IL: Moody, 2004).

[72] Michael Papesh, Clerical Culture (Collegeville, MN: Liturgical Press, 2004), 74-75.

[73] Rev. Jay Biber, "Preparing Seminarians for an Emerging Paradigm of Priestly Leadership," Seminary Journal (Spring 2003), 47.

[74] John Paul II, Pastores Dabo Vobis, no. 16.

[75] O'Donnell, "The Anatomy of a Vocation," 75-79.

[76] Biber, "Preparing Seminarians," 48.

[77] Robert Leavett, SS, "The Formation of Priests for a New Century," Seminary Journal (Fall 2002), 15.